The Young Angler's Handbook

The Young Angler's Handbook

Brian Morland

Hamlyn
London · New York · Sydney · Toronto

Acknowledgements

Photographs
Hamlyn Group – John Howard, 8; Brian Morland, 34/35.

The publishers would like to thank **Gerry's of Wimbledon** for the use of their premises and tackle for the photograph on page 8.

Special thanks are due to ANGLING TIMES for the use of all other photographs.

Illustrations by
Ray and Corinne Burrows; Linden Artists Limited – Jim Channell and Richard Smith; Keith Linsell.

Published 1980 by
The Hamlyn Publishing Group Limited
London   New York   Sydney   Toronto
Astronaut House, Feltham, Middlesex, England.

ISBN 0 600 30409 4
Printed in Italy by Interlitho

Contents

Introduction

Whilst writing this book for young anglers I came to the conclusion that the best way to introduce it was to recall my introduction to angling.

I was fortunate to live in an area where there were plenty of clean rivers and streams. As far back as I can remember I was fascinated by the fast-flowing water and the deep, mysterious pools. Long before I owned a fishing rod I spent many hours exploring the river and learning at first hand about the life which abounded in and around the water. School holidays were spent by the side of the river catching bullheads, crayfish and stone loach from under the rocks in the shallow margins. I used to watch and catch by hand the strange looking lampreys which every April massed by their thousands in the shallow water to spawn. In the company of other youngsters I spent many hours catching minnows and small gudgeon in jam jars lowered into the river on lengths of string.

When I was eventually given an old fishing rod my imagination had already been fired. My early efforts at rod and line fishing were restricted to a stretch of water where the fishing was poor, but free. The river was teeming with gudgeon and I became very adept at catching these. Very occasionally I would catch a small chub or grayling and these red letter days were remembered for a long time. My angling apprenticeship was long but the lessons learned were well remembered. I was not fortunate enough to be taken fishing by experienced anglers very often but I read a great deal about the subject in books.

Learning to catch fish is a very gradual process and there is no substitute for experience. There is no such thing as an instant angler. The most important thing young anglers should remember is that fish are wild creatures and as such are easily frightened by bankside disturbance. You will never catch many fish if you have scared them all away before you start fishing. Fishing is such a complex subject that no one knows all the answers. Some anglers will always catch more and bigger fish than others. That is the way of life. The important thing is that you enjoy your fishing. Many anglers eventually specialize in different aspects of the sport, some, for instance, preferring match fishing whilst others are only interested in fly-fishing for trout. It matters very little provided you gain enjoyment and satisfaction. In this book I have attempted to cover the basic methods for catching fish. As you gain experience, some of these methods can be refined to suit circumstances you will encounter.

I hope that young anglers new to the sport will gain as much pleasure and satisfaction from angling as I have received over the years.

Tackle requirements for float fishing

A really good tackle shop offers a wide range of rods, reels and sundry tackle items

Three piece fishing rod

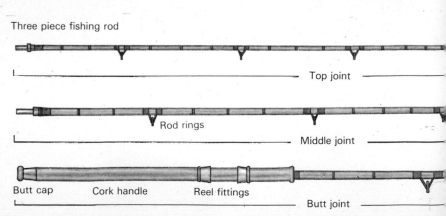

Top joint

Rod rings

Middle joint

Butt cap   Cork handle   Reel fittings

Butt joint

Although most anglers begin fishing by learning to float fish I shall also include several items of basic equipment in this chapter which are needed for other methods of coarse fishing.

Rods

Choosing a good rod for float fishing can be very confusing for the beginner as there are so many different types available. There are basically two methods for catching coarse fish: one is float fishing and the other is legering. I have yet to find a satisfactory general purpose rod. A rod with a through action (one whose curvature is extended throughout the whole rod) designed for float fishing can be used for light legering whereas a leger rod is not practical for float fishing. As a general guide for the beginner, float fishing rods are between 12 feet (3·7 metres) and 14 feet (4·3 metres) long whilst leger rods are 10 feet (3 metres) or less. A 12 foot (3·7 metre) glass fibre rod is light

enough to be handled by a ten year old and will enable him to control his tackle more easily than using a short rod. Some 12 foot rods have a through action whilst others have only a tip action which enables a very rapid strike to be made. For the beginner or young angler, however, a medium to through action rod will prove more versatile.

One word of warning when buying a fishing rod: avoid some of the

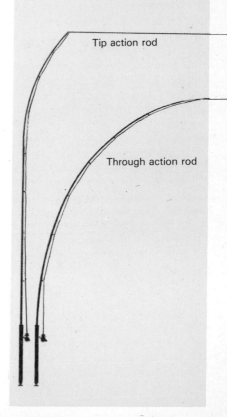

Tip action rod

Through action rod

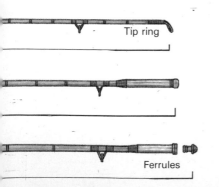

Tip ring

Ferrules

short, so-called 'boys' rods' which are sold. These are very often useless and you are better off saving the money. Most young anglers gain some experience at fishing by using tackle passed down from friends or relatives before actually buying a new fishing rod. Many youngsters show an interest in fishing and, although a few lose this interest after a short time, the remainder become addicted for the rest of their lives. It is wise during this period of initial interest to use handed-down tackle to make sure that the interest in fishing is not just a passing phase.

A fishing rod is not cheap so it is worth the little bit of effort required to keep it in good condition. If it happens to be raining when you finish fishing, wipe the rod down with a dry cloth before putting it back in its bag. Most rod bags have a small tag sewn on to the bottom and the safest way to store a rod between fishing trips is to hang it on to a wall by this tag. Periodically wipe the rod over with a cloth covered in Vaseline. Spigot ferrules on a rod can wear slightly and if this happens just rub the spigot taper with the end of a wax candle. The wax coats the spigot so that it makes a snug fit in the ferrule. The rod rings can have grooves worn in them by the continual passing through of line so these need checking at least once a season. If you do not look after your rod it could well let you down at the moment you least want it to – for example when you hook that fish of a lifetime!

Reels

For coarse fishing there are three types of reel to choose from. Two of these, the fixed-spool reel and the closed-face fixed-spool reel, are very similar. The fixed-spool reel is the most versatile reel used by anglers and they can be bought for a very modest price. The spools on the front of these reels can be changed very quickly, enabling the angler to change over to heavier or lighter lines without changing reels. It is important when using fixed-spool reels to fill the spools with line correctly. Two types of spool are available with most reels. One is a shallow spool for use with lines up to 3 lb (1·4 kg) breaking strain and the other is a much deeper spool for heavier lines. Line can be wound on to the shallow spool directly and no problems will occur when casting. With the deeper spools even the heavier breaking strain lines need backing underneath to fill the spool correctly. An easy way of doing this is to simply build up the well of the spool with insulating tape. When correctly filled the line should be about 1·5 millimetres below the front rim of the spool. This ensures that when casting the line flows off the spool easily. If the spool is underfilled the line will drag across the rim of the spool, seriously interfering with the casting of light tackle. Underfilled spools are one of the commonest reasons for anglers being unable to cast satisfactorily.

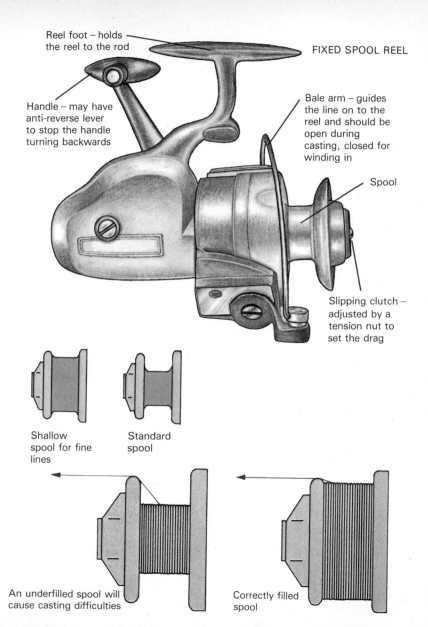

Reel foot – holds the reel to the rod

Handle – may have anti-reverse lever to stop the handle turning backwards

Bale arm – guides the line on to the reel and should be open during casting, closed for winding in

Spool

Slipping clutch – adjusted by a tension nut to set the drag

Shallow spool for fine lines

Standard spool

An underfilled spool will cause casting difficulties

Correctly filled spool

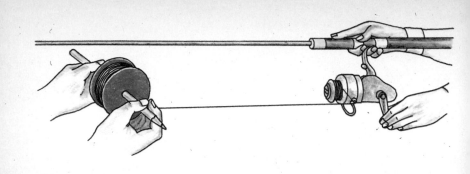

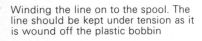

Winding the line on to the spool. The line should be kept under tension as it is wound off the plastic bobbin

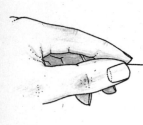

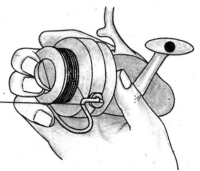

Fixed-spool reels

Fixed-spool reels need very little attention provided they are kept clean and free from grit or mud. The two parts which are most likely to wear are the bale arm roller and the bale arm spring. Spares are readily available from the manufacturers and these parts are easy to change. The closed-face fixed-spool reel is very similar to the standard fixed-spool reel except that the spool is enclosed in a metal housing. The line is fed out from the reel through a hole or a circular groove at the front of this housing. The press button release mechanism enables one-handed control of the casting.

For the beginner there is not a lot to choose between these two reels although the closed-face type is not really suited for fishing for big fish since they cannot take heavy line, nor do they allow back-winding.

Above: Closed-face fixed-spool reel

Below: Centre pin fly reel

Centre pin reels

Centre pin reels are not widely used, and the beginner is better off using a fixed-spool reel. For the expert float angler the centre pin reel is a joy to use as it gives much better control under certain fishing conditions. There is also more direct control and contact with a hooked fish using this type of reel. Casting is severely restricted with a centre pin reel and for this reason I advise any beginner to purchase a fixed-spool reel.

Line

There are many brands of fishing line to choose from and these are sold on 100 metre spools. For float fishing the beginner should choose a line with a breaking strain of 2 lb to 3 lb (0·9 kg to 1·4 kg). Anglers have personal preferences for brands of line but there is not a lot of difference in quality between the leading brands. Nylon line is very durable but it should still be checked regularly for signs of wear and fraying. The breaking strain of a line can decrease after a while especially if exposed to extreme weather conditions. It is a wise precaution to check the strength of the last few metres of line for weakening before tackling up.

Floats

The wide variety of floats is often bewildering for the beginner. There are hundreds of different shapes and sizes to choose from. A float is used for two main purposes. The first is to enable casting and presentation of a bait to the fish in such a way that the fish accepts the bait as a natural offering. The second reason is that the float acts as a very effective bite detector to the angler. Contrary to what some anglers believe, fish do not try to pull the float under. This is purely the result of a fish picking up the bait.

There is a float designed for just about every situation. Brightly coloured floats look attractive and there is a tendency for anglers to collect floats in the way that some fly anglers collect artificial flies. The majority of anglers have many more floats than they actually use. Start collecting floats for the particular type of water you are going to fish and then begin adding to your collection as and when you need them. For float fishing in flowing rivers stick floats, balsa floats and avon floats are used. Waggler floats are now widely used in flowing water but it is advisable for beginners to get plenty of practice trotting a bait down with a stick float before attempting to fish wagglers. In very slow flowing rivers and lakes, antenna and windbeater floats are the best type. Always remember that these special floats are only a refinement and that an experienced angler

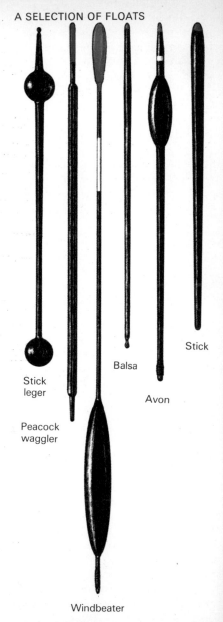

Stick

Balsa

Stick
leger

Avon

Peacock
waggler

Windbeater

will catch plenty of fish using a simple porcupine quill for a float. Modern floats are usually marked with the amount of split shot needed to cock them. These figures are not always accurate; to check them fasten a length of line to the float, add the shot and test in a bucket of water. Some floats are rather fragile – especially the longer antennae and waggler floats – so they should be kept in a separate container to avoid damage. A long plastic tube with two end caps is ideal.

Lead shot

The split shot for loading floats can be either bought loose or in plastic containers which hold about six different sizes. The cheapest way is to buy the split shot loose so that only the required size is bought, and no shot is wasted. The five sizes which will cover most eventualities are swan shot, AAA, BB, No. 1 and No. 4 in order of size. Some lead shot is very hard and I much prefer the softer variety. With the softer shot the split in the shot can be prised open with the finger nails and the shot moved along the line or else taken off altogether. There is no need to squeeze the shot on to the line really hard as this will damage the nylon. Use just enough pressure to prevent the lead moving along the line during casting and striking. Shot which is squeezed on to the line by too much pressure causes the nylon to flatten and is a potential weak spot when

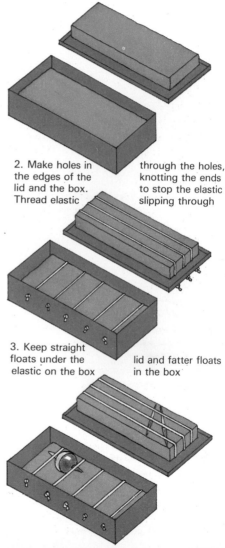

HOW TO MAKE A FLOAT BOX

1. Glue pieces of foam rubber to the inside of a plastic box and its lid, leaving a space around the edge of the lid.

2. Make holes in the edges of the lid and the box. Thread elastic through the holes, knotting the ends to stop the elastic slipping through

3. Keep straight floats under the elastic on the box lid and fatter floats in the box

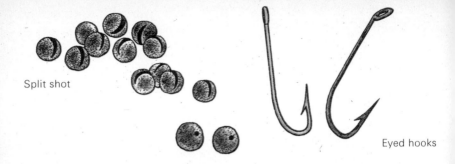

Split shot

Eyed hooks

playing a good fish. Most anglers clamp the split shot on to the line using their teeth and this is quite satisfactory providing you do not swallow the shot or bite through the line! Do not try moving the position of the shot on the line without prising the shot open because if the line is not actually broken by doing this, it will be drastically weakened.

Hooks

Far too many anglers insist on only using the smaller sizes of hook for all their fishing. By doing this they are putting unnecessary restrictions on their chances of hooking and landing good fish. The size of hook used should be chosen to suit the size of bait, and the species of fish to be caught. If you restrict all your fishing to tiny hooks and tiny baits then probably all you will catch will be tiny fish. Hooks for freshwater fishing range in size from a size 1 down to size 20. The higher the number then the smaller the hook. Hooks smaller

than a size 20 are available but these are ridiculously small and the beginner is best advised to forget them. Most anglers begin fishing by using maggots and are not really particular about what species of fish they catch, so hook sizes 14, 16, and 18 will suffice for this purpose.

The actual type of hook to be used poses a difficult problem. Eyed hooks are the cheapest but in the smaller sizes they are slightly more cumbersome than a spade end hook of the same size.

Tying hooks to line

Spade end hooks can be bought loose or already tied to a length of nylon cast. The hooks already tied to nylon are very expensive for the young angler and my advice is to learn how to whip your own spade end hooks on to nylon. The spade end knot is not an easy knot to learn but it is well worth the effort. Avoid trying to tie one of these knots at the waterside when your hands are covered in groundbait or fish slime. Buy a spool of nylon line with a slightly lower breaking

Spade end barbless hook

strain than the reel line you use for float fishing and make up several hook lengths before your fishing trip. If a 2 lb (0·9 kg) breaking strain line is normally used then a 1½ lb (0·7 kg) breaking strain line is used for the hook length. The reason for this is that should your tackle become snagged or else you hook a fish you cannot handle, the short hook length will break before the reel line and all you will lose is the hook. Tie the spade end hook on to this lower breaking strain line using a spade end knot and then cut the nylon to leave a 0·5 metre length attached to the hook. Form a loop on the end of the hook length with a three-turn loop knot and store the completed cast in a cellophane hook packet ready for use. Always ensure when tying a spade end knot that the nylon is on the front of the flattened hook shank and not on the outside otherwise the spade end will fray the nylon.

For the hooks larger than a size 14, eyed hooks are ideal and can be tied direct to the reel line using a clinch knot. When using eyed hooks always check that the eye is fully closed before tying them on to the line.

Barbless hooks

Barbless hooks are the best type of hook to use in the smaller size range. The main reason for this is that if a little care is taken they can eliminate any hook damage to a fish. With a barbed hook there is always a small mark left in a fish's mouth and if a fish is unhooked hurriedly or clumsily the fish can be badly damaged. Another great advantage of using barbless hooks is that they are much sharper and consequently hook penetration is much easier. My only doubt about advising beginners to use barbless hooks is that fish have to be played on a tight line. If the line is allowed to go slack whilst playing a fish then the hook is liable to slip out. Eventually, I would like to see every angler converted to barbless hooks when using the smaller sizes. Far too many young fish are damaged when being unhooked and grow into maturity with deformed mouths.

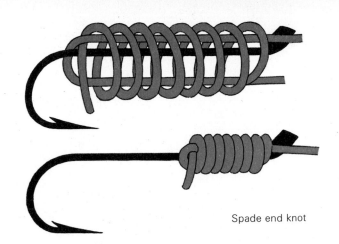

Spade end knot

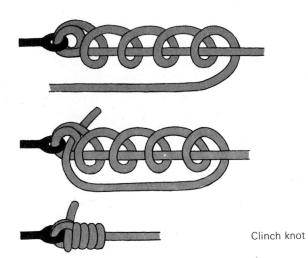

Clinch knot

Three turn loop knot

Method of joining hook length to reel line

Triangular

Pan net

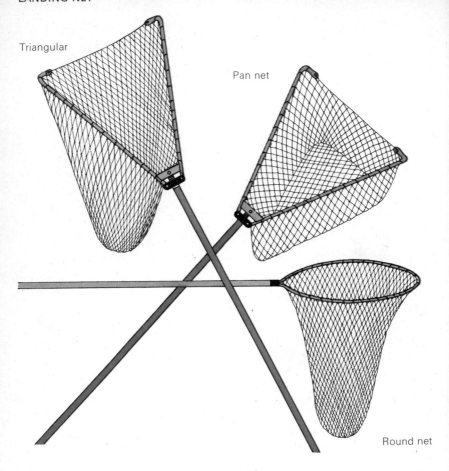

Round net

Angling accessories

The following accessories are not required for float fishing alone; they will be useful for all the types of fishing that you decide to pursue. They are included in this chapter simply because most young anglers will begin by float fishing, and will thus probably read this advice before moving on to other types of fishing.

Landing nets

An adequate landing net is really an essential item of tackle. Small fish can be lifted out of the water, but fish over $\frac{1}{2}$ lb (0·22 kg) should be netted out. A good sized frame is essential as it can be quite frustrating trying to coax a big fish into a tiny landing net! A triangular shaped net has the advantage over a circular one in that it makes it easier to land fish in shallower water. The modern pan shaped landing nets are ideal for small to medium sized fish in that they are shallow and you do not have to grope around in the mesh for your fish as you do in a deep net. As you gain experience you will need a larger, deeper landing net for species such as pike, carp and barbel. Landing nets are now available in fine, knotless mesh and these avoid a lot of fish damage. The only disadvantage with a fine mesh landing net is that they are more difficult to manoeuvre in a fast flowing river. Even so, I prefer this type to the wide mesh knotted nets because as many torn tails and fins are caused by landing nets as by keepnets.

Keepnets

Whilst not an essential item of tackle, many anglers like to retain fish in a keepnet until the end of the day. If you take up match fishing then a keepnet does become essential for holding fish until the weigh-in at the end of the match. The knotless keepnets have helped tremendously to avoid damage to fish but they are not infallible. There is not much point in going to all the effort of retaining fish in a knotless net if, at the end of the day, you tip the fish

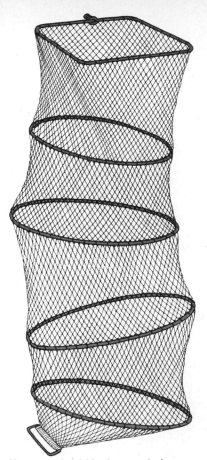

Keepnets should be large and of a knotless material

on to a patch of gravel or mud. Many water authorities now insist that knotless nets be used and have laid down rules governing minimum sizes. Try to choose a large, wide keepnet. The width of the keepnet is nearly as important as the length, for the fish must have room to move.

Pike gag (note the protective corks on the sharp prongs)

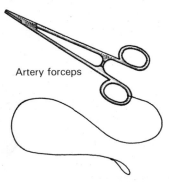

Artery forceps

Miscellaneous items

The type of tackle box you use is entirely a matter of personal preference. The fishing basket is still popular and is used as a seat as well as a tackle carrier. The disadvantages of baskets are that they are heavy, and riverbanks are not always conveniently flat enough for them to be used as a seat. A large rucksack will hold most of your tackle and you can carry a lightweight chair to sit on. For long fishing sessions the back rest on a fold-up chair makes for more comfortable fishing.

All sorts of containers can be used for storing the smaller items of tackle such as hooks and floats. Hooks kept in small tins will be blunted from being rattled around and are best kept in a lined hook wallet.

A strong rod holdall is handy for transporting rods and protecting them from damage.

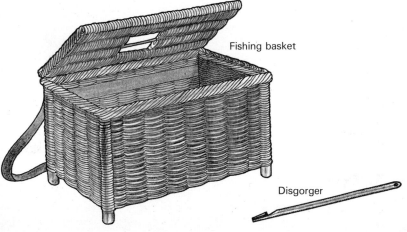

Fishing basket

Disgorger

Although not essential, a large fishing umbrella is a good investment. The umbrella is as useful for blocking off a cold wind as it is for keeping you dry. In very windy weather the umbrella should be staked down with guy ropes otherwise you could find it taking off. Fishing in winter without an umbrella can be a pretty miserable experience.

A small but handy item of tackle is a disgorger. For the small hook sizes a narrow disgorger with a hollow conical end is the best type. Avoid the types with a forked prong at the end. For larger hooks, and for dealing with sharp toothed fish such as pike, you will need a pair of artery forceps.

Once you have acquired the basic tackle necessary for float fishing, the rest can be accumulated over the years.

Adjustable rod rests

Bait box

Fly wallet

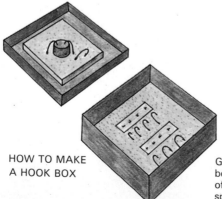

HOW TO MAKE
A HOOK BOX

Glue some foam rubber inside a plastic box and its lid. Glue a cork in the middle of the lid. Push hooks into the cork and sponge. Different sizes can be labelled

Float fishing tactics for rivers

Choosing the swim

In a flowing river the fish are seldom evenly distributed and it is worthwhile spending some time looking around to find the most likely spots. The ability to determine the best fish-holding areas is something which increases with experience. Weather conditions, water conditions, and seasonal movements of fish all have to be taken into account when choosing where to fish. The beginner is unlikely to be bothered about selectively fishing for a specific species of fish but with experience it is quite possible to choose areas of river more favourable to one species.

Weedbeds and
bridge supports –
perch

Fast flowing water –
dace, gudgeon,
roach

Gravelly river
beds – gudgeon

Shallow water near
the bank – minnows

Reedbeds –
pike

Deep water with a
muddy bottom – bream

LIKELY PLACES TO CATCH FISH IN
RUNNING WATERS

Deep pools —
barbel, chub

Overhanging trees and bushes,
and tree roots — chub

Take note of any bankside features
which affect the flow of the river such
as overhanging willow bushes, gravel
spits or stakes reinforcing banks. In a
spate river, the river bed can alter
suddenly from sand or fine gravel to
large rocks. The time of day also
plays a very important part in fish
location. During the summer months
species such as chub and barbel will
often venture into shallow water
towards evening when the light
begins to dim. Fishing is such an
unpredictable sport that it is impossible to give any exact information as to where fish will be found.
The ability to 'read the water' and
seek out the best fishing can only
come with experience.

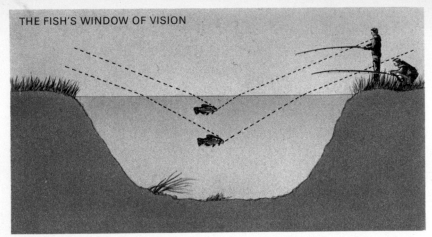

THE FISH'S WINDOW OF VISION

A fish lying deeper in the water has a better view of the bank than one lying near the surface. An angler keeping low at the water's edge is less likely to be detected than one standing upright

Tackling up

Once you have decided which swim you are going to fish you can begin to assemble your tackle. Do this away from the water's edge and then you are unlikely to scare any fish which may be near the bank. If the banking is very high and devoid of cover do not stand on the top of this or you will be outlined against the sky and will scare away all the fish in the vicinity. When you remove the rod from its cloth bag put away any rubber caps, which protect the ferrules, into your pocket so you do not lose them. Fit the rod sections together and then glance along the length to check that all the rod rings are correctly lined up. Fit the reel on to the rod handle about six inches (15 cm) away from the top of the handle and secure it in

position with the winch fittings. Ensure that the centre of the reel is lined up with the bottom ring of the rod. Press a rod rest into the ground and lean your rod against this whilst threading your line. Open the bale arm of the fixed-spool reel and thread the line carefully through all the rod rings.

Selecting the type of float to suit the swim you are fishing is very important. For turbulent, strong flowing water you need a float which is capable of carrying a lot of lead shot, such as an avon float or a balsa float. In a steady, smooth glide a stick float will be ideal. The strength of flow in the river and the depth dictates the amount of buoyancy needed in the float. Assuming that the chosen swim is not very turbulent or fast flowing, select a stick float and

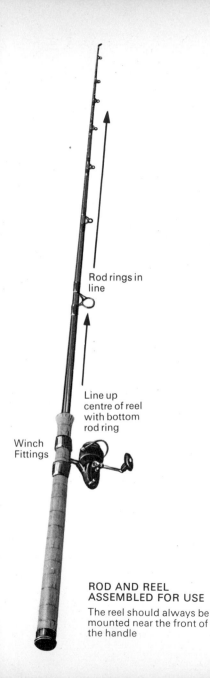

Rod rings in
line

Line up
centre of reel
with bottom
rod ring

Winch
Fittings

**ROD AND REEL
ASSEMBLED FOR USE**

The reel should always be
mounted near the front of
the handle

attach it to your line with a float rubber at both the top and bottom of the float. Slide the float carefully up the line and form a loop at the end of the line using a three-turn loop knot. A size 16 hook will be ideal for using with maggots as bait, and after tying the hook to a nylon hook length, fasten it through the loop in the end of the reel line. Give the line a steady tug to ensure the knots are secure. The split shot is then nipped on to the line between the float and the hook length. If the current is strong then the bulk of the shot should be well down towards the hook length. In a steady flow the shot can be spaced out evenly along the line in groups of progressively lower weight towards the hook. Set the float at the depth you consider the swim to be at the spot where you have chosen to fish. Fasten the hook to the bottom rod ring and reel in to tighten your tackle and line against the rod. Leaving the rod propped against the rod rest, begin assembling your keepnet and landing net. Place your keepnet in the edge of the river making sure there is sufficent depth of water to cover the mesh and that the net is not in too strong a current. Quietly carry the rest of your tackle down to the water's edge, taking advantage of any bankside vege-tation. Arrange your seat and tackle so that you can fish without having to move about to reach items. Ideally, you want to be able to hook, land, and place a fish in your keepnet without moving from your seat.

Casting

Fixed-spool reels make casting a simple operation but skill is required to achieve pin-point accuracy and distance. Casting should be effortless, so for distance fishing the float and lead shot should be heavier to achieve the length of cast without strain. The overhead cast is probably the most widely used technique except where you are hampered by a steeply rising, overgrown bank. Grasp the rod handle in your right hand at a point just above where the reel is fastened. Pull back the bale arm on your reel and trap the line against the spool with your forefinger. Grasp the butt end of the handle with your other hand and bring the rod back over your shoulder. To cast, push forward with the hand which is next to the reel and pull your other hand, bringing the butt of the rod in towards you. As the rod moves forward from the vertical position release the line trapped by your forefinger against the reel spool. The line will flow easily from the correctly filled spool sending your tackle out across river. Follow through with the rod so that it ends

CASTING WITH A FIXED SPOOL REEL

1. Open the bale arm and trap the line against the rim of the spool with your forefinger
2. Raise the rod back over your shoulder making sure that your tackle does not become entangled in bankside vegetation
3. Bring the rod forward sharply and release the line (see inset) trapped by your finger when the rod is approximately in the 10 o'clock position. The amount of force required to cast the tackle depends on the distance from the bank you want to cast. If you need a great deal of effort to achieve your distance then your tackle is too light and you should change to a heavier float with more shot

up slightly below the horizontal position.

As soon as the tackle alights on the water, trap the line against the reel spool once more. If the cast is well made, the float will land gently in the desired spot. The object is to lob the tackle out rather than throw it. The exact moment you release the line from the reel with your forefinger is important. Too soon and your float will head skywards, and too late will send your tackle crashing into the water in the wrong place with a resounding splash which will scare away the fish.

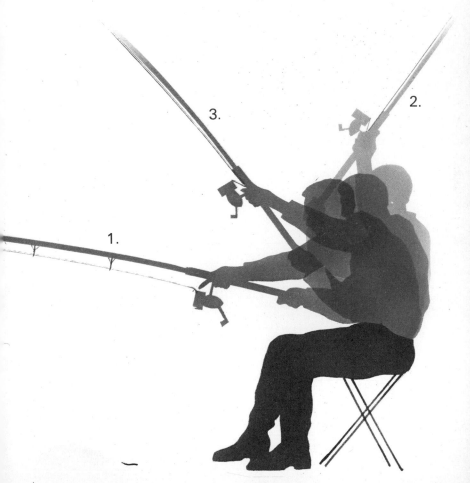

Where distance casting is not required, a gentle sideways cast, using just the one hand holding the rod next to the reel, will suffice. On overgrown stretches of river sideways casting is necessary to avoid catching the hook in the undergrowth. When you have made a cast, snap the bale arm on your reel back into position, making sure your knuckles are out of the way. In winter, when your hands are cold, rapped knuckles can be very painful! The procedure for casting with a closed-face fixed-spool reel is similar, but instead of trapping the line against the spool of the reel you simply press the central button to release the line at the correct moment. Casting accurately can soon be mastered with practice providing you aim for accuracy first before progressing to distance.

Trotting

In this type of float fishing, the bait is allowed to travel down a section of river at the pace of the current. Before actually beginning to fish, the depth of the water you are fishing should be established. In a flowing river this is easily done without having to cast around with a heavy plummet. Set the float to the depth you imagine the swim to be. When the water is fairly clear you can see the bottom for a little way out so this is not difficult to do. Cast out to where you intend to swim the bait down with the current and let the flow of the water carry the float

downstream. Adjust the float up the line with each cast until the float begins to drag under. This will happen as soon as the hook begins to catch on the river bed.

Once you have found the depth you can set about catching some fish. Throw a few loose maggots into the line of current down which you intend to trot the float. This attracts fish into the area. Do not be tempted to heave in great quantities of ground-bait all at once. Adopt a 'little and often' principle with loose maggots being fed into the swim every few casts. Cast out into the head of your swim and leave the bale arm open. As the current takes your float downstream, control the speed at which it travels by gentle pressure

An angler controlling his float whilst trotting for roach

with your forefinger on the line as it leaves the open spool of your reel. Hold the rod fairly high so that as little line as possible is in contact with the surface of the river. Begin by trotting your tackle with the bait touching the bed and then if the fish begin to rise up in the water to intercept your loose feed you can reduce depth. The float can be left to travel down at the speed of the current or it can be held back slightly by checking the line leaving the open reel with the forefinger. When the float dips under the surface, trap the line against the rim of the spool with your forefinger and strike by moving your rod in a sideways arc. As soon as the hook is struck into the fish, engage the bale arm of the reel with a quick turn of

Above: This angler strikes after allowing his float to travel at the speed of the current

Below: The path of a float when trotting a river

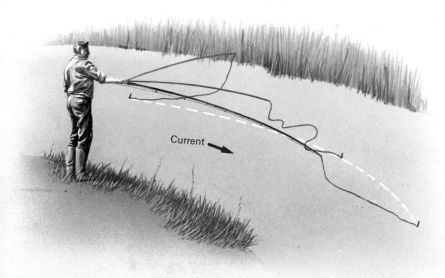

Current

the reel handle. When you have hooked a fish, reel in as you bring the rod back into the normal position to play the fish to the bank. Do not strike and then suddenly lower the rod as this will slacken the line and may well cause the hook to spring loose. Keep in contact with the fish at all times. To play the fish towards the bank, keep the rod tip fairly high and try to lead the fish gently away from the rest of the shoal without too much disturbance. When you are trotting a float down with the current try to strike with a sideways, upstream sweep of the rod rather than a vertical strike. If you are fishing in fairly shallow water and you strike vertically you will force the fish towards the surface and the resulting splashing may disturb the rest of the shoal.

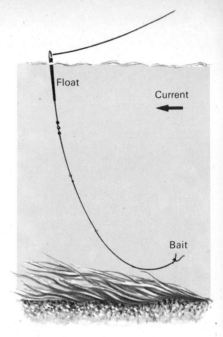

Above: When allowed to travel at the speed of the current the float will always precede the bait

Below: Mending the line by rolling the rod tip

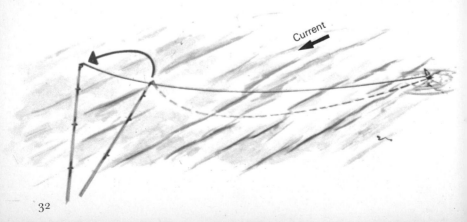

As soon as you strike into a fish, release the anti-reverse lever on your reel so that you can backwind if the fish is large enough to power across into the middle of the river. If you hook a really powerful fish such as a barbel, which will swim away very quickly indeed, simply release the anti-reverse lever and let go of the reel handle. When the fish dashes across the river it will be able to pull line from the reel causing the handle to spin round backwards. As the fish slows down you can then catch hold of the reel handle again to begin playing the fish back towards the bank. Failure to release the anti-reverse lever may result in the first powerful rushes of a large fish breaking your line.

When trotting a float down the current the line should be fairly straight between the rod tip and the float. Sometimes the wind or cross currents will cause the line lying on the water surface to bow and this needs straightening. This is known as 'mending the line' and is achieved by rolling the rod tip sharply in a small arc to straighten the line without dragging the float out of position. You should be in contact with your float all the time it is travelling down with the current.

Laying on

There are a number of occasions when fish will accept a stationary bait yet will completely ignore a moving one. To present a stationary bait at a distance, you must leger – a method of fishing we will look at later – but for fishing close to the bank you

When trotting, the length of swim fished can be extended by casting further upstream and allowing longer travel downstream. With such a long cast, once the float is caught by the current, line must be retrieved on to the reel as the float approaches you and fed out again as it travels away from you

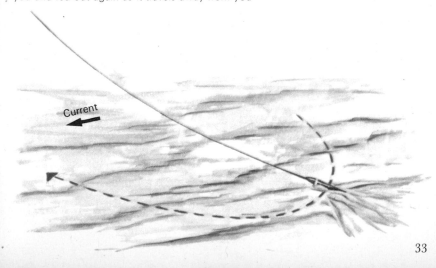

Current

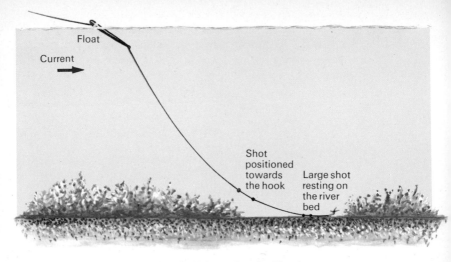

Float

Current

Shot
positioned
towards
the hook

Large shot
resting on
the river
bed

Above: Laying on over depth in a river. A good method in winter

can employ a method known as 'laying on'. In winter when the water temperature is very low and the fish are not prepared to move for a bait this method can be very effective. For laying on, position the shot well down the line towards the hook, with a large shot which will be resting on the river bed. Set the float so that you are fishing well over depth. Cast out across the current and then place the rod on two rests. The current will swing the tackle round until it comes to rest immediately downstream of your rod. Bites can vary quite a lot, and because you are fishing with a very tight line between the rod tip and the float, a strong bite may pull the tip of the rod over. If no bites are forthcoming after ten minutes or so, you can reel in a couple of turns to

draw your tackle a few centimetres upstream. The float should be long and slim and fixed to the line both top and bottom. A fat-bodied float will create too much resistance to the surface current.

Stret pegging

This method is very similar to laying on. The float is set well over depth with the shot lying on the river bed. The tackle is cast directly downstream and the line tightened up. By raising the rod tip a fraction, the weight on the river bed can be eased downstream a little way before coming to rest again. Keep the line between the rod and the float under tension at all times. By continually lifting the rod tip and letting line out the tackle can be very slowly moved downstream. This is a very good method of searching for fish when the river is high and coloured, such as after heavy rains.

Waggler floats

In recent years waggler floats have been used a great deal in match fishing. I have seen many youngsters

Below: Laying on at the side of the main flow produced this chub on a raw winter day

An angler hooks a good fish after wading out to avoid thick marginal weedbeds

buying this type of float and then using them in completely wrong situations simply because they have read that a leading matchman had won a big competition using a waggler. Waggler is the name given to a type of float which is attached to the line by the bottom end of the float only. A waggler float is designed to carry a lot of weight so you can present a bait to fish at a great distance and avoid tangles when casting. The float should be fastened on to the line by passing the line through the ring at the bottom of the float and locking it in position by nipping a couple of large shot either side of the ring. These shot should be spaced about one centimetre apart. Whatever loading the float will carry, the bulk of the shot should be placed next to the float and the rest distributed down the line towards the hook.

For fishing in a wide, smooth-flowing river a straight waggler should be used, and in a very slow-flowing, fenland river or drain, a bodied waggler is used. Fishing a bodied waggler in a very sluggish river is virtually the same as using an antenna float in a lake. Because they are attached to the line by the bottom ring only, wagglers can normally only be fished through the swim at the speed of the surface flow. This means that the float always precedes the bait. Always try to cast across and slightly downstream when using these floats as it makes line control much easier. For fishing close to the

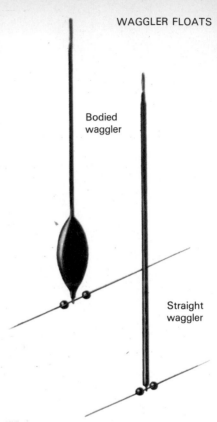

Bodied waggler

Straight waggler

bank, tackle control is easier with a stick or a balsa float.

Bites

A shoal of fish lying in the current and facing upstream do not have to move about a great deal to find food. The current brings the food to the fish which only have to move slightly to one side or upwards to intercept the food particle. If you feed the swim with loose maggots the fish pick

36

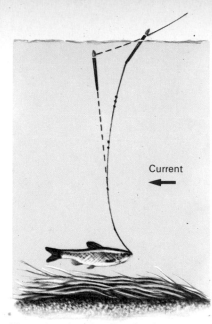

them up as they are washed down in the current. When a bait is presented on or close to the river bed a fish feeding in this way will not pull the float under. What happens is that the fish snatches the bait and the float continues to travel down until the line tightens between the hook and the float and the force of the current pushes the float under. The faster and shallower the river you are fishing then the faster this happens. In deep rivers with a steady flow there is always a slight time lapse between the fish intercepting the bait and the float dragging under. When you are fishing over depth there is often no noticeable difference between a bite and the hook dragging on the river-bed, so if you are in any doubt always strike.

Above: In a river there is a time lapse between the fish intercepting the bait and the float going under

Below: Four different bites in a stillwater yet only one has pulled the float under. Strike at any unusual movement of the float.

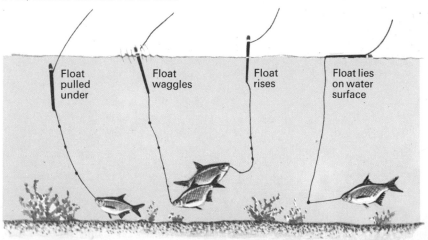

Float pulled under

Float waggles

Float rises

Float lies on water surface

For ideal bait presentation in flowing rivers the rate at which the float is allowed to travel down the river should be a lot slower than the surface current. This is achieved by controlling the rate at which the line leaves the spool of your reel with your forefinger. The reason for doing this is that the surface water speed of a river is considerably faster than at the bottom. This is more noticeable in deep water than in the shallows. If, in a deep, swift river, you allowed the float to travel down at the same speed as the surface current the hookbait would be dragged far too quickly along the bottom. Many anglers mistakenly believe that when you slow down the rate at which the float travels down the swim, you are allowing the baited hook to travel

down ahead of the float. This is not so, and all you are doing is allowing the bait to travel through the swim at the normal speed of the current near the river bed. The variation in speed of flow between the surface and the river bed is very marked, and in times of extra water can often cause anglers to ignore a swim which is full of fish, because they wrongly assume that the flow is equally fast on the bottom.

You will often see pictures in books and magazines showing what happens when you hold your float back in the current, and most of them are wrong. The line will not form a forward curve towards the baited hook and the bait will not be waving enticingly under the noses of the waiting fish, as is so often stated. The line immediately below the float will

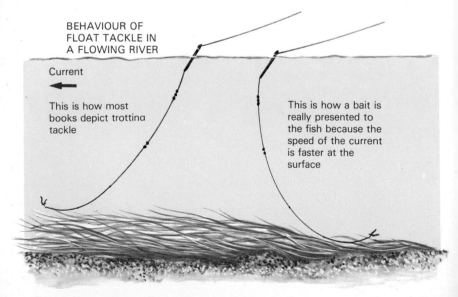

BEHAVIOUR OF
FLOAT TACKLE IN
A FLOWING RIVER

Current

This is how most books depict trotting tackle

This is how a bait is really presented to the fish because the speed of the current is faster at the surface

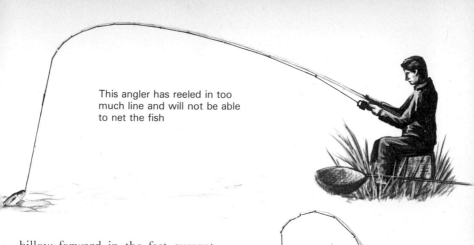

This angler has reeled in too much line and will not be able to net the fish

billow forward in the fast current, but will curve backwards nearer the river bed where the bait is being dragged along in the much slower current.

Landing a fish

Many fish are lost off the hook just as they are being landed, so it is important to land your fish properly. As the hooked fish begins to tire, draw it towards the bank. Sink the landing net in the edge of the river at your feet. Draw the fish across the surface by keeping the line tight and raising the rod until the fish is over the top of the sunken net. Raise the landing net smoothly with your free hand so that the fish is trapped in the mesh. You can now lower the rod on to a rod rest and lift the net out of the water with both hands. Do not try and chase the fish with the net, or try and lift the fish over the rim of the net or you could snap the line.

A lot of beginners have difficulty in

By raising the rod and back-winding the fish can be brought within easy reach of the net

Below: When landing a big fish the net needs to be grasped near the frame to support the weight

Above: The correct way to land a fish. The net is submerged and the fish is drawn over the net

drawing the hooked fish across the surface towards the bank. A common mistake is to keep the rod too low when playing the fish and then reeling in the line until the float jams in the top rod ring. If you have reeled the float too close to the rod tip to be able to raise the rod and skim the fish across the surface towards the bank, simply allow the reel to backwind and raise the rod at the same time. Whilst you are doing this it is imperative that you keep the line under tension. Very heavy fish cannot be lifted straight out of the water by lifting the landing net handle. Keeping the mouth of the net above the surface, pass the handle through your hands towards you until you can lift the frame of the net.

Float fishing tactics for stillwaters

Lakes can be the most difficult or the easiest of waters to fish. I will try to explain this contradiction. In a river the areas which hold the most fish are not difficult to determine because of the strength of the current and the contours of the banking. When float fishing in a river the float travels down with the current and so covers quite a large area of water. In a lake

An angler float fishing alongside beds of water lilies in a lowland lake on a hot day

the float stays where it is cast out and consequently the bait is only presented in one tiny area. Choosing a good swim to fish is therefore very important in lake fishing. On large lakes and gravel pits there are often areas of water which for one reason or another seldom hold any fish. It stands to reason that when fishing a lake the choice of swim is very important. In small lakes with a healthy fish population, or in a good swim in a large lake, the fishing can be very easy at times. Another fact which makes float fishing a lake

LIKELY PLACES TO CATCH FISH IN STILLWATERS

Fallen trees –
tench, bream,
carp, eels

Open water – bream

Reedbeds –
pike, perch

Muddy bottom
with water lilies –
tench, bream, carp

Gravel bottom
with water plants —
roach, rudd

Shallow water
near the bank —
minnows

easier than a river is that tackle control is simpler. In a stillwater it is unnecessary to continually mend the line to keep in contact with your float. As you gain experience your ability to spot the signs of a good swim will improve. Do not always assume that the swims which are obviously well fished are the best spots. Quite often these swims are fished regularly for the simple reason that they are nearest the car park. Some anglers are loath to walk any distance and just stop at the nearest stretch of water.

Setting up

When you have chosen the particular swim you are going to fish you should begin tackling up well away from the water's edge. Fish frequently patrol the margins of a lake and you should try to avoid any unnecessary disturbance. The first job to do is to stake out your keepnet. Creep up to the water's edge and, by inserting your landing net handle inside your keepnet, quietly push it out into the water. Heaving the net out will disturb fish over a wide area. By placing the net in the water before beginning fishing you are giving the swim a chance to recover from the disturbance whilst you continue to tackle up. Don't wait until you catch your first fish before throwing your keepnet out or you will disturb the

PLACING A KEEPNET IN THE WATER WITHOUT CREATING A DISTURBANCE

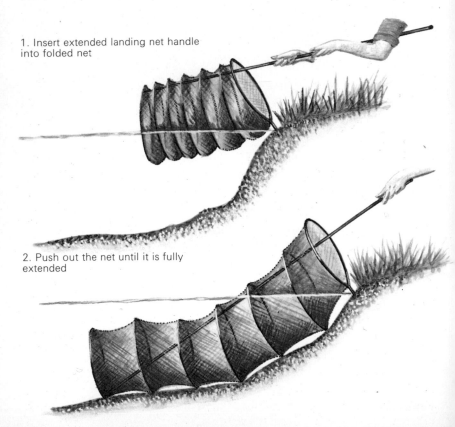

1. Insert extended landing net handle into folded net

2. Push out the net until it is fully extended

When drawing a big fish over the landing net don't be tempted to snatch at the fish

rest of the shoal – unless you are fishing well out from the bank. Before tackling up is also a good time to soak your ground bait with water. Screw the landing net into the handle so that it is ready should you hook a sizeable fish first cast. Assemble the rod, fasten the reel in position and thread the line through the rod rings, taking care not to miss any.

Finding the depth
The next important task before actually fishing is to thoroughly plumb the depth of your swim to find out how deep it is. Fasten a quill float on to your line with two rubber bands, one at the top of the float and one at the bottom. Nip a couple of swan shot on to the end of the line or else just sufficient shot to make the float sink. The swan shot makes much less disturbance in your swim than does a heavy, specially designed plummet being continually cast around. Approach the water's edge, slide the float up the line to the depth you imagine the water to be, and cast out into the area you intend fishing. If at the first attempt the float disappears then slide it further up your line to increase the depth. Alternatively, if the float lies flat on the surface then slide it down the line to reduce the depth. The correct depth is determined when the float sits with just the tip showing above the surface. Explore the water in front of you very thoroughly to find out if the depth is

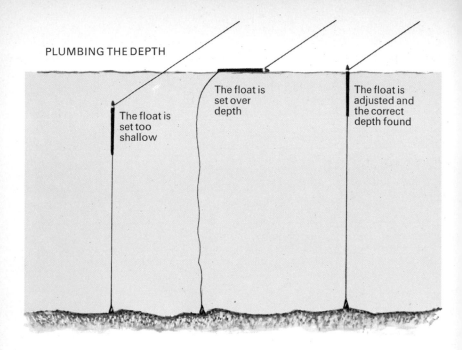

The float is
set too
shallow

The float is
set over
depth

The float is
adjusted and
the correct
depth found

even, or if there are any ledges or deep holes in the lake bed. It can be very important to know the exact depth of water you are fishing as sometimes a few centimetres can mean the difference between a good catch of fish or no fish at all. Gravel pits which have been excavated with mechanical diggers can have a very varied bottom and without this knowledge fish location can be difficult.

When you have discovered the depth of a swim by adjusting your float, swing the tackle towards you and catch hold of the swan shot on the end of the line. Hold the swan shot against the end of your rod handle in front of your reel and then reel in the slack line so that the float tightens up against the rod. Note the position of the float against the rod rings on the rod. Starting from the end of the handle count the number of rod rings until you reach the tip of the float. The water level in a lake seldom fluctuates a great deal so you now have a float setting for every time you fish that particular swim. The exact measurement doesn't matter provided you can recall the number of rings along the rod for fishing the float. If your memory is not very reliable then make a note of the number for that particular swim in a diary. If you fish the lake frequently then you can soon build up a list of the exact float settings for several swims and dispense with having to plumb the depth again.

Once you have plumbed the depth of the swim slide the swan shot off the end of your line and replace them in your box for future use. Remove the quill float from your line and choose a suitable float for the day's fishing.

Tackling up

The antenna float with a bulbous body and a long narrow stem will be ideal for most stillwater applications. Pass the line through the small ring in the bottom of the float and let the float slide loose along the line. Form a loop in the end of the reel line using the three turn loop knot. For the

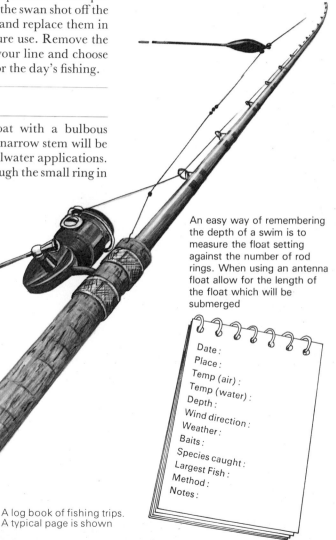

An easy way of remembering the depth of a swim is to measure the float setting against the number of rod rings. When using an antenna float allow for the length of the float which will be submerged

Date :
Place :
Temp (air) :
Temp (water) :
Depth :
Wind direction :
Weather :
Baits :
Species caught :
Largest Fish :
Method :
Notes :

A log book of fishing trips. A typical page is shown

Antenna floats should always be fished by attaching the line to the bottom end only

Above: This angler has organised all his tackle within reach so that he doesn't have to move

beginner who is going to use maggots as bait choose a size 16 hook which you should have already tied to a length of nylon cast and attach this to the reel line as shown on page 19. Stick the hook point into the end of the cork handle in front of the reel and turn the reel handle to gently tighten the line. Prop the rod against a rod rest or tackle box and slide the float along the line until it is level with the rod ring marking the depth of your swim. Take a couple of large split shot and nip one either side of the float ring leaving a slight gap between them so that the float is not held too tightly. The size of the split shot depends on the amount of

weight your float will carry. Ideally the bulk of the shot should be directly beneath the float.

Before placing the rest of the shot on the line quietly move the tackle to the edge of the chosen swim. Try and arrange your seat and all your tackle so that you can reach everything without having to stand up. Unless you have chosen a very inaccessible bank you should be able to play, land, unhook and place your fish in the keepnet without having to walk about. Position your rod at your side on two rod rests so that the handle is within easy grasping distance. The front rest should be lower than the back one so that the rod is tilted

Below: A fine tench is drawn towards the submerged rim of the landing net

By undershotting, more of the float will be visible in rough conditions

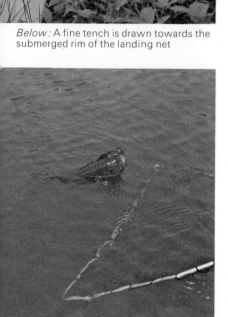

towards the water and the rod tip is submerged.

Complete the shotting of your float, keeping the shot in groups and reducing the size of the shot towards the hook. Place a small 'tell-tale' shot about 4 cm away from the hook (the reason for this will be clear a little later). If you have set the depth of your float correctly this shot should be resting on the lake bed with all the other shot well up the line. In windy weather when the surface of the lake becomes ruffled with small waves, the float can be undershotted so that more of the antenna will be showing above the surface. In really choppy conditions or when fishing at long range use a windbeater float which is a large antenna with an enlarged brightly coloured bob built into the tip for easy visibility. The length of antenna float you use depends a great deal on the effect of the weather on the lake surface. Wind blowing along an exposed area of the lake can cause the surface layer of water on a nearby, sheltered area of the lake to drift. This surface drift is frequently in the opposite direction to the wind. The idea of using a long antenna float which has all its buoyancy built into the bottom of the float is to sink your line below this surface movement. As a general rule the windier the weather then the longer the antenna float you should use. In calm conditions a shorter antenna float can be used and shotted down so that just the tip is visible above the surface.

The colour of the float tip can also be important. Choose a colour which is clearly visible against the reflected light on the water surface. On dark, cloudy days a bright orange or yellow float tip will show up best, and on clear calm days a float with a black or dark tip may be more visible.

Bite detection

Cast your tackle beyond the area you intend to fish and draw the float back to the required position. To do this allow the float to cock and then dip the rod tip below the surface and wind in the line. This will draw the float back and at the same time sink the line below the surface. You can then place the rod on the two rod rests so that the rod tip remains submerged. For the beginner who is not really particular about the species of fish he catches, a couple of maggots will attract most species likely to be found in a lake. A small amount of breadcrumb groundbait and a few handfuls of loose maggots tossed round the float will help to entice fish into the area of the baited hook.

An antenna float used as I have described is a very sensitive tackle rig and the type of bite which is registered by the float can vary quite a lot. Strike at any movement of the float which appears suspicious. A fish picking up your bait from the lake bed will not necessarily cause your float to disappear under the surface. Your float will only disappear when a fish picks up your bait and swims away. This is the reason for having the tell-tale shot near your hook. When a fish just gently tilts forward and picks up your bait it will lift this shot off the bottom. This reduces the load on your float and it will rise slowly up out of the water. If the fish then moves off with your bait the float will glide across the surface and gradually sink from view. When using small baits such as maggots, strike as soon as you notice the float rising up out of the water or else the fish may eject the bait or be deeply hooked. If you have baited up a very small area, the fish don't have to travel very far to pick up another free

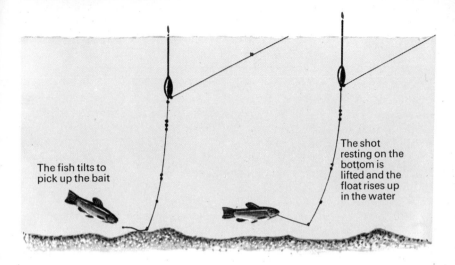

The fish tilts to pick up the bait

The shot resting on the bottom is lifted and the float rises up in the water

offering. In winter, when the water temperature is very low, the fish are likely to move around even less so the bites are unlikely to be very positive. Do not make the mistake of assuming that bites which hardly move the float are from shy fish – a shy fish will suck in a bait and eject it faster than you can blink. These bites, which are often encountered on stillwaters, are from confidently feeding fish which don't dash away with the bait. In calm conditions it is easy to see any slight movement of your float but when the surface is rough and wind-swept these delicate bites become more difficult to notice.

Large baits for positive bites

One simple way of encouraging fish to give more positive bites is to increase the size of your bait. There is

a very subtle reason for this. Fish, like all wild creatures, have a number of inbuilt instincts which help them to exist. In times of food shortage it is the creatures which manage to find the most food which remain the fittest and survive. This instinct is so strong that it remains even when food is plentiful. A classic example of this instinct which everyone can observe is displayed by garden birds. Spread some breadcrumbs on the lawn together with a number of larger pieces of bread and watch the re-action of the sparrows and starlings. The birds will eat the breadcrumbs where they find them but will drag the larger bits of bread well away from the main feeding area so that they can eat the bread without it being stolen by a rival. This is exactly what happens with fish. A shoal of fish confidently feeding over a carpet of maggots will suck them into their mouths at once. If one of them finds a larger item of food it will grab it and bolt from the shoal to avoid competition and so register a tearaway bite on the float. Therefore you will normally obtain a much more vigorous bite using a large bait than a small one. This problem is seldom encountered whilst float fishing a flowing river because a fish can intercept a bait without moving, yet the force of the current will push the float under to register a bite.

Detecting bites with antenna floats

The antenna rig I have described for stillwaters will be suitable for most situations but can be varied slightly for special applications. Begin by fishing on the bottom but if you are continually throwing in loose maggots round your float the fish may begin rising up to intercept them. Move most of your shot to just below the float and the tackle will then fall slowly through the water. This is known as fishing 'on the drop' and is often a highly successful way of catching rudd and roach. In lakes where they thrive, tiny rudd can become a pest. On warm summer days the surface may become a mass of rudd fry and if you are to catch any better quality fish you may have to get your bait down past the rudd very quickly. To do this move the bulk of the shot down the line so that the bait is dragged through the shoal of rudd before they have time to grab it.

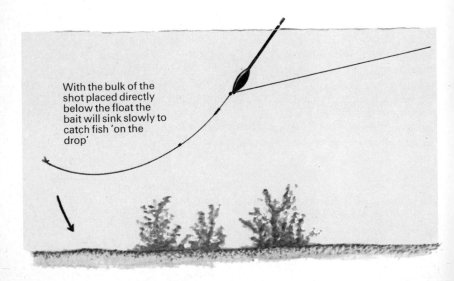

With the bulk of the shot placed directly below the float the bait will sink slowly to catch fish 'on the drop'

If the wind is really strong you may find that even when using a very long antenna float your tackle is being dragged slowly across the surface. To avoid this remove the small tell-tale shot next to the hook and replace some of the smaller shot on the line with a larger one placed about half a metre away from the hook. To ensure that this larger shot is well on the bottom move the float further up the line. Before moving the float do not forget to open the slits in the split shot or the line will snap. The larger shot resting on the bottom of the lake will act as an anchor for the tackle.

During the summer months the fish in lakes are very active but as the water begins to cool down in the autumn, location becomes more important than ever. In cold water fish become reluctant to move even for food and a number of species refuse to feed at all except on the milder days. Float tackle for detecting bites on a lake in winter should be extremely sensitive. An antenna float with a very thin insert in the top of the stem is a good investment. Set the depth of the float so that the bait is just touching the bed of the lake but no line or shot are touching. The bait should be small, such as a single maggot, caster, or even a tiny piece of bread flake. Shot the float so that only enough of the insert remains above the surface to enable you to see it clearly. On really calm days when

A fish is hooked using a long antenna float to combat the effects of a strong breeze

the surface is unruffled and you are fishing fairly close to the bank you can shot the float so that only the surface tension is holding it up. This is probably the most sensitive tackle rig you could use. A fish only has to nudge the bait to register a bite.

Lake fishing in winter can be a waiting game but there are ways of searching an area of water for fish. Cast out your tackle and leave it in one spot for ten minutes. If no bites are forthcoming then slowly reel in a couple of turns on the handle. Repeat this every few minutes as you gradually draw the tackle back towards the bank. Bites often occur as soon as you stop winding the reel. The fish tend to shoal in small areas in winter so when you do get a bite concentrate on that area. Don't be tempted to

An antenna float shotted for delicate fishing in flat calm conditions

By using an antenna float and submerging the rod tip, the line can be sunk to overcome surface drift in windy conditions

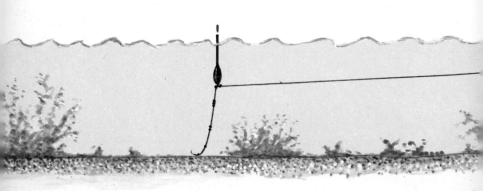

throw in a lot of heavy groundbait but scatter a few hook samples around your float. Bites in cold weather can register as little more than a slight lifting of the float or a gentle sideways movement, so strike at the slightest sign.

As you gain experience in lake fishing this float rig can be modified slightly to selectively catch the larger species of fish such as bream, tench and carp. For these species, especially tench and carp, you will need to use a heavier breaking strain line and larger hooks. Use a larger bait so that you are not continually catching small fish. Float fishing a lake is not as active a pastime as fishing a flowing river but it is extremely interesting and at times very rewarding.

A mixture of carp, tench, roach and bream

Tackle requirements for legering

Legering is a technique used for catching fish which are feeding on or close to the bottom of the river or lake without using a float to register the bites. In most instances the bait is anchored to the river or lake bed by a lead weight, but in flowing rivers the lead can be allowed to roll along the bed to search for feeding fish. When a fish picks up the bait the line is pulled and the bite is registered by the rod tip moving. The rod tip is not very sensitive, so there are now many devices which can be fitted to the rod tip or used to detect line movement between the reel and the first rod ring.

Rods

In chapter one I mentioned that a 12 foot (3·6 metre) float rod with a through action can be used for light legering. For the beginner who is restricted to just one rod this is the best compromise but to seriously begin using leger tactics to catch some of the larger species of fish then a second rod is a necessity. Just as there are many different types of float rod, there are numerous leger rods many of which are designed for a special form of legering. Most leger rods are between 9 feet (2·7 metres) and 10 feet (3 metres) long. The type of leger rod you choose depends a great deal on the type of fishing for which you intend to use the rod. A light, wand-like rod with a built-in quiver tip would be no use for dragging a reluctant barbel or chub from amongst the roots of a riverside willow bush. Similarly a Mk IV carp rod is far too strong for catching small bream from a wide, featureless fen-land river.

If you intend to leger for the larger species of fish such as chub, barbel, tench and carp, a Mk IV carp rod or similar action rod is ideal. These rods can be used for a wide range of applications and if you choose one of glass fibre, they are very light yet are capable of dealing with most species of big fish.

For fishing in slow moving rivers or lakes, or for smaller species of fish, a much lighter type of leger rod can be used. Many of these are designed for use with a swing tip bite indicator attached to the rod end. Most, if not all of them, will have a special tip ring which has a threaded hole in the end for fastening a swing or quiver tip bite indicator. Avoid buying your first leger rod with a quiver or swing tip built into the rod. This will severely limit the use of the rod. Swing tips are fine when fishing a slow moving river or lake for bream but are useless on a fast moving river.

Reels

Fixed-spool reels are without question the best type of reel to use for legering. Of the two types of fixed-spool reel, the standard open-faced reel is better for legering than the closed-face reel. Some closed-face reels have no facility for backwinding and this is necessary when legering for both adjusting bite indicator settings and playing large fish.

When legering with a fixed-spool reel it is important to have the anti-reverse lever engaged when striking. If you fail to do this the force of the strike will cause the reel to backwind and line will be released from the reel reducing the impact of the strike, resulting in the hook failing to penetrate the fish's mouth. Whilst legering for powerful, large species of fish such as barbel and carp, the clutch on the reel should be very carefully set before fishing. After tackling up you should fasten your line to a fence post or some other solid object and walk some distance away, paying out line as you go. Close the bale arm, engage the anti-reverse check on your reel and tighten up on the object to which you have fastened your line. Bend the rod by heaving on the rod handle as if you were applying pressure to a big fish and adjust the clutch so that line is paid out well before the breaking point of the line is reached. This is a safety measure so

Set the clutch by tying the line to a post, tighten up and adjust the clutch to give line before the breaking point is reached

that if you strike far too enthusiastically into a big fish, the clutch will slip and prevent the line snapping. As soon as you strike into a fish when legering, release the anti-reverse lever on the reel so that you can backwind when a fish makes a powerful run. By backwinding and setting the clutch you have two measures for preventing a powerful fish from breaking the line.

Line

The strength of the line used depends on the size of fish you are trying to catch and the weight of the terminal tackle you use. Lines used for legering should be stronger than lines used with float tackle. You cannot cast a one ounce (28 gramme) leger weight using a 2 lb (0·9 kg) line as the force exerted to cast the weight will snap the line. A very experienced angler may be able to fish with this combination but the beginner will run into all kinds of problems. When using light leger tackle in slow moving rivers for species such as bream and roach, a line of 3 lb (1·36 kg) breaking strain is adequate. For chub and barbel fishing in a fast river using big baits, you should use a line of at least 5 lb (2·25 kg) breaking strain.

Leger weights

There are a number of different types of leger weight to choose from. The shape and size of leger you use is governed by the distance you need to cast, the speed of the current, the nature of the river bed, and the buoyancy of the bait you intend to use.

The most widely used leger weight is the *Arlesey bomb*. This pear-shaped leger with a swivel set into the narrowest end of the lead was developed to enable anglers to cast long distances whilst fishing particular types of water. This type of leger can be used as a free running lead by passing the reel line through the eye of the swivel or by tying the leger on to a sliding link.

DIFFERENT TYPES OF LEGER WEIGHTS

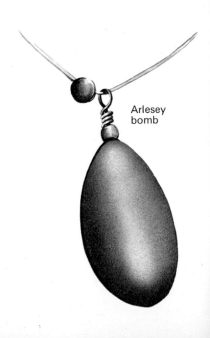

Arlesey
bomb

A *link leger* is the most versatile of all leger rigs. It is simply a length of nylon line which is tied at one end on to a small diameter split ring or a swivel. The other end of the line is tied to the swivel in the top of an Arlesey bomb or else swan shot are nipped on to the nylon link. The link is attached to the reel line by passing the line through the split ring or the top eye of the swivel. The link is then free to slide along the line. A swan shot link leger is the most versatile leger you can use. The weight can be adjusted in seconds by sliding one of the swan shot off the end of the nylon link or by adding more swan shot. This way you can change from static legering to rolling legering without having to change your terminal tackle. The swan shot link leger is extremely useful when fishing over a gravelly or rocky river bed. Should the swan shot become firmly trapped between rocks a steady pull will slide the shot off the nylon link and free your tackle. A standard leger weight trapped amongst rocks could well result in you losing all your terminal tackle. The length of the nylon link you use depends on how you want to present the bait. Where the river bed

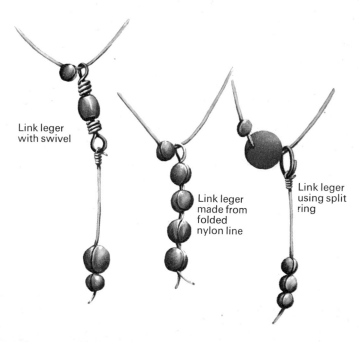

Link leger
with swivel

Link leger
made from
folded
nylon line

Link leger
using split
ring

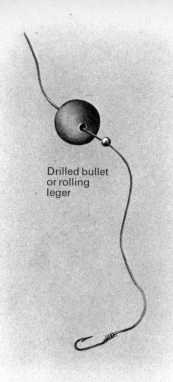

Drilled bullet
or rolling
leger

is gravelly, a long link with just one or two swan shot will enable you to present a static bait even in a very fast flow. The long link will trail behind the bait and the swan shot will become trapped amongst the gravel and hold the bait in position.

A quick and simple way of making a link leger is to fold a length of nylon double to form a small loop and nip swan shot over the folded lengths of nylon. The reel line is passed through the nylon loop formed in the link.

The *drilled bullet* is a round ball of lead with a hole through the centre. The reel line is passed through this hole. This type of leger is used for allowing a bait to roll along the river bed with the current. In most instances a swan shot link leger or a small Arlesey bomb will work just as efficiently.

The *coffin lead* is so named because of its shape. It is a flat lead and was designed to present a static bait in a

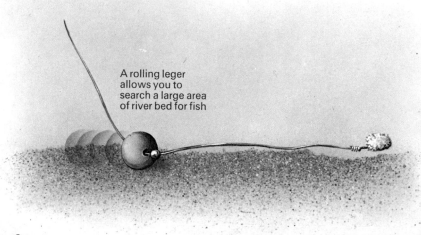

A rolling leger
allows you to
search a large area
of river bed for fish

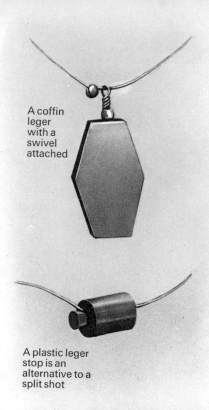

A coffin leger with a swivel attached

A plastic leger stop is an alternative to a split shot

fast flowing river. The shape of the lead offers very little resistance to the current. The line passes through a hole drilled through the centre of the lead. These leads offer considerable resistance to a taking fish because of the line passing through the centre. A great improvement when using a coffin lead is to insert a small swivel into the central hole of the lead and squeeze this into position, leaving the end ring of the swivel protruding. The reel line can then be passed through this swivel offering less resistance to a taking fish.

The leger is fixed the required distance from the hook by a split shot nipped on to the line. An alternative method of doing this is to use a plastic leger stop. A leger stop is simply a short piece of plastic tube through which the reel line is passed and a tapered plastic peg is inserted trapping the line against the inside of the tube. Leger stops have the advantage

When a fish picks up the bait the line is pulled through the leger

An open ended swimfeeder

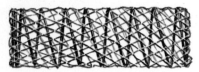

Hair curlers can be made into swim feeders

A bait dropper for feeding maggots into the swim

1.

2.

over split shot by being easily moved along the line to alter the distance between the leger and the hook. They are also less likely to slip down the line when casting large legers than are split shot.

Swim feeders

These are sometimes used instead of legers to hold the bait on the bottom. A swim feeder is a plastic tube with holes through the walls of the tube. A weight is incorporated into the tube and the swim feeder is attached to the reel line in a similar manner to leger weights. The feeder is usually crammed with maggots which, after the tackle has landed on the river bed, crawl out through the holes and form a carpet of loose feed to attract fish into the vicinity of the baited hook. The advantage of using a swim feeder is that it concentrates groundbait in the exact spot it is required. Most feeders are designed to be used with maggots but some are open ended and can be filled with cereal

MAKING A SWIM FEEDER
1. Punch big holes in a small plastic tube with scissors
2. Tie on a small nylon loop and wrap wire around one side to weight the tube
3. Pack the feeder with bread or other bait

3.

groundbait. Swim feeders can be bought in a large range of sizes. The larger ones create a lot of disturbance when they hit the water and used in the wrong situation will frighten more fish than you catch.

Bite detectors

Swing tips

The swing tip is a bite indicator used when legering and is attached to the special end rings on the rod. A small metal adaptor is screwed into the end ring of the rod and attached to this adaptor is a short length of rubber tube. The swing tip is then fastened into the other end of the rubber tube. When the leger tackle has been cast out, the rod is placed in the rod rests and the line is wound in until it tightens between the rod tip and

leger. The swing tip, which is hinged at the end of the rod by the rubber tube, will fall back so that it hangs down at right-angles to the rod. Wind in a little so that the tip then inclines slightly towards your leger tackle. A fish which picks up your bait and moves away from you will cause the swing tip to lift up. Should a fish decide to swim towards you the tip will fall back suddenly into the vertical position.

Many match anglers use rods with the swing tip built into the rod but this restricts the use of the rod to special situations. Swing tips are best suited for lake fishing and in very slow moving rivers. In stronger flows the force of the current will straighten the tip out so that it does not serve its purpose. Slight increases in flow can be overcome by using a

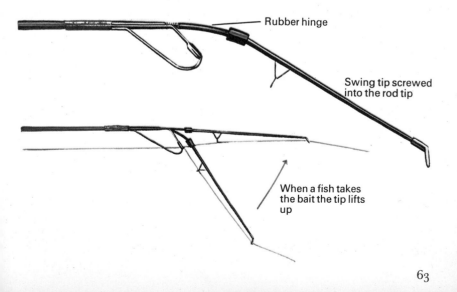

Rubber hinge

Swing tip screwed into the rod tip

When a fish takes the bait the tip lifts up

stiffer rubber hinge but there is a limit to the speed of current you can fish effectively using a swing tip. The major problem young anglers encounter when using a swing tip is in casting. No angler can cast as accurately and easily with a swing tip dangling from the end of the rod as they can without one.

Swing tips were originally developed for bream and roach fishing in wide fenland rivers and lakes where the leger tackle is cast well beyond the feeding fish and then drawn back into position. By overcasting and then drawing back the tackle you can correct any slight inaccuracy. Learn to cast leger tackle

A swing tip correctly used. The angler is ready to react to the slightest movement

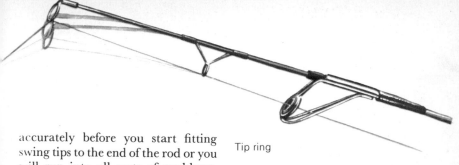

Tip ring

A quiver tip fitted into the screwed tip ring of a rod

accurately before you start fitting swing tips to the end of the rod or you will run into all sorts of problems. Windy weather can also cause problems when you are trying to detect bites by watching for movements on the swing tip. One way to overcome this is to shelter the tip from the wind. Some anglers do this quite successfully by placing a thin sheet of clear perspex mounted on to a bank stick alongside the swing tip, so that it cuts out the wind. Some of these boards have a series of lines etched in them so that the slightest movement of the swing tip against these lines can be noticed. These are known as target boards. Used in the right circumstances swing tips are a very sensitive form of bite detector for legering.

Quiver tips

The quiver tip is really a sensitive extension of the rod. Like the swing tip, the quiver tip can be screwed into the end ring of the rod. The quiver tip is a length of tapered glass fibre with two or more additional rod rings whipped to it. This tip is much more sensitive than the rod end and bites are detected by this sensitive tip pulling over when a fish takes the bait. Quiver tips are best used in

flowing water and there are a wide selection of tips available in different lengths and thicknesses to suit most situations. Obviously a much more sensitive tip is required to detect bites from roach and dace than is needed for barbel in a strong current.

Accurate casting is not impaired nearly so much with a quiver tip as it is with a swing tip. After casting out, the line is tightened up and the angler watches the tip for any sign of movement from a taking fish.

It is worth remembering that both quiver tips and swing tips are only methods for detecting bites. The most important aspect of legering is ensuring that your baited hook is in the right spot and that it is presented correctly. There are other methods of detecting bites when legering, but because these do not involve particular items of tackle produced for the purpose, they will be described in the next chapter.

Leger tactics for rivers & stillwaters

Legering is a skilful method of catching fish if used correctly and should not just be used as a last attempt after failing to get any bites using float tackle. There are many situations where legering will not only catch you more fish but much bigger ones as well. In fact it would be true to say that more specimen fish are caught by legering or variations of legering than any other method.

Legering for big fish

I have used the term big fish rather than specimen fish on purpose. A two pound chub is not a specimen chub but it is a big fish and will put a good bend in your rod when you hook one. There are several important reasons why legering is such an effective method for catching the larger species of fish. Most of the larger species feed on or near the river or lake bed. Barbel, tench, bream and, to a large extent carp, are all bottom feeders and this is where it is necessary to present the bait. All these fish will occasionally feed nearer the surface and carp will often accept a surface bait, but for consistent success the bait has to be where the fish feed most of the time, and that is on the bottom.

The most important reason why legering for the larger species of fish is so successful is that it allows the presentation of a bait which is extremely attractive to the big fish but is immune from the unwanted attentions of the smaller ones. To do this it is unnecessary to use a really large bait, rather one which cannot be nibbled away by the small fish. The tackle used has also got to be strong enough to withstand the powerful fight put up by the fish when it is hooked. This is especially true if you are fishing water which is full of weed or sunken trees which you must prevent the fish reaching. Presenting a large bait using strong line on float tackle has lots of problems, especially in a flowing river. Long float rods are not designed to be used with strong lines and a rod of 12 feet (3·6 metres) designed for float fishing is not powerful enough to drag an angry barbel away from a sunken tree root. The stronger nylon line is, the thicker the diameter and the less flexible it becomes. When using a stronger line, bait behaves in a less natural way because the nylon is not flexible enough. Legering overcomes this problem because the line near the hook lies on the bed of the river or lake and is not affected by the current. In a fast flowing river, especially one that is fairly shallow, it is not easy to present a bait acceptable to big fish on float tackle. Barbel and chub will not often chase a bait dragged through at speed with the current but will accept an offering trundling along the bottom using a rolling leger.

Touch legering is the most sensitive method for detecting bites whilst legering

Legering also enables you to anchor a bait in places – such as a small gap between overhanging willow branches on the opposite bank of a river – which are impossible to reach with a float. In a lake or pond it is acceptable to present a large bait on float tackle at close range. Use an antenna float attached by the bottom end only and fish over depth so that the bait is well on the bottom. Fishing at long range, however, does require the use of leger tackle for ease of casting. There are no hard and fast rules to determine where and when to leger for the larger fish, but try and take into account the weather and water conditions. To consistently enjoy catching the larger species of fish, have an open mind and do not restrict your fishing to one method or bait.

Touch legering

Touch legering is the most sensitive method of detecting bites. After casting out and tightening up, the rod is held and bites are detected by holding the line between the fingers. There are several ways of doing this and you should choose one which is comfortable to you. When bites are expected soon after casting out, the rod can be held in one hand and bites felt for by lightly holding the line between the reel and first rod ring with the finger and thumb of the other hand.

If you are using a large bait such as a lobworm and you need to give a taking fish some line, simply pull the line you are holding a little way to the side of the rod. When you feel a fish drawing on the line, allow the hand which is holding the line to move back towards the rod and then strike. The rod can be held more easily if you support the handle against your body with your elbow.

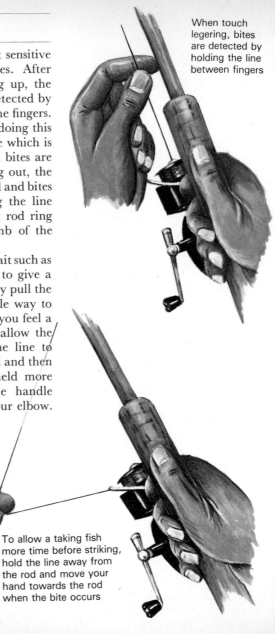

When touch legering, bites are detected by holding the line between fingers

To allow a taking fish more time before striking, hold the line away from the rod and move your hand towards the rod when the bite occurs

When legering the rod should be supported on a grooved rod rest

Should you find it uncomfortable to hold the rod for any length of time then support it on a rod rest, still keeping hold of the handle. The rest should be the deep grooved type to prevent line becoming trapped between the rest and the rod. Touch legering using just one hand can be practised by letting the line pass from the reel and over the forefinger of the hand which is holding the rod. By using your fingers to detect bites you can sense the slightest movement on the line. Occasionally a fish will only mouth the bait without moving away and the only indication of this is a slight trembling on the line. Touch legering is the only method which will register this type of bite, although it does have its limitations and few anglers can hold a rod steady for any great length of time even if it is supported on a rest. In winter it is not much fun trying to touch leger with an icy wind gradually numbing your fingers. Its use is also restricted to flowing rivers where the pull of the current keeps the line taut.

A grooved rod rest allows for the free passage of line

Touch legering using one hand. The line passes over the forefinger for bite detection

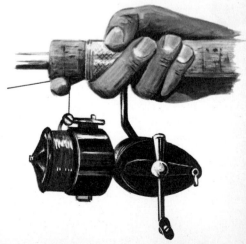

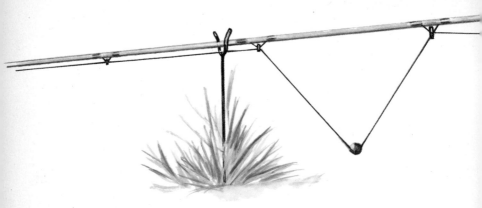

Bobbin indicators

There are many variations of these but they are all based on the same principle. The simplest idea of all is the dough bobbin. The idea behind using a dough bobbin is to allow a fish to move away with a bait without feeling any resistance and to indicate to the angler what is happening. After casting out, the rod is placed in two rod rests with the back rest, supporting the handle, raised higher than the front one. Ideally the rod tip should be pointing directly at the bait, but in a river this is not always possible. A piece of bread paste is moulded on to the line between the first and second rod rings. The line and bobbin are then pulled down towards the ground. When a fish picks up the bait and moves away it will draw line, pulling the dough bobbin up towards the rod. The

amount of line you give a fish is controlled by how far away from the rod you pull the dough bobbin. In windy weather, which causes the bobbin to swing about, the rod should be positioned just clear of the ground and the dough bobbin pulled on to the ground to one side of the rod. When a fish bites, the bobbin will trundle along the ground before shooting up to the rod. The dough bobbin will fly clear when you strike, or it may wedge against a rod ring and should then be pulled clear. Do not put the dough bobbin on to the line between the reel and first rod ring because if it does not fly clear on the strike it will jam on to the spool messing up the line and hindering following casts. The strength of the flow in a river limits the use of a dough bobbin. If the flow is too strong the force of the current will simply pull it up towards the rod no

A dough bobbin indicator for detecting bites whilst legering

In windy weather the bobbin can be pulled down to the ground

matter how big a bobbin you use. It is, however, a very cheap and effective method of detecting bites when legering.

Rolling leger

The idea that legering is a static form of fishing is not true. In a flowing river a swim can be explored just as effectively with a leger as it can with a float. The type of leger which will allow the bait to trundle along the river bed depends a great deal on the nature of the bottom. For example, a drilled bullet is ideal if the river bed is sandy. Choose a weight which just holds its position in the current but will begin to roll along as soon as you lift the tip of your rod. Cast across the river and allow your tackle to settle on the river bed. If no bites are forthcoming, raise the rod to set the leger trundling along until it comes to rest again. Hold the rod all the time and touch leger by holding the line between the finger and thumb. In this way it is possible to feel, through the line, the actions of the leger rolling along the river bed. The leger will gradually work down and across the river until it reaches the nearside bank downstream from where you are fishing. The next cast can be made slightly downstream of the first, searching a fresh area.

On gravelly sections of river a swan shot link leger is better than a drilled bullet and will hold bottom easier with less weight. In a really fast flowing, weedy river, a rolling leger can enable a bait to be presented in

A rolling leger can be worked across the river and under streamer weed in search of fish

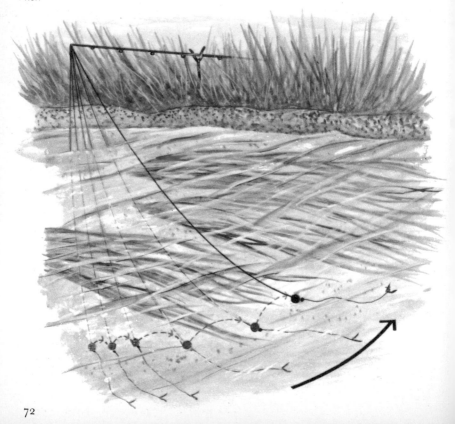

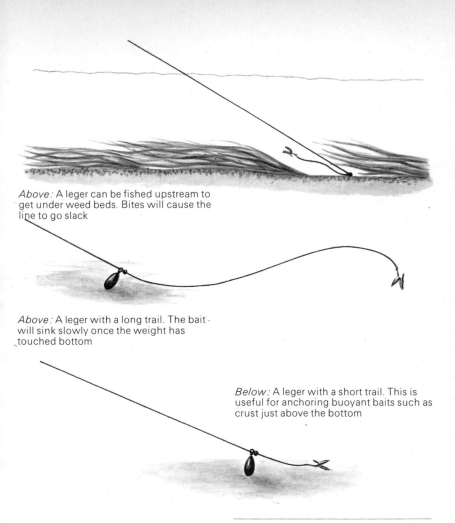

Above: A leger can be fished upstream to get under weed beds. Bites will cause the line to go slack

Above: A leger with a long trail. The bait will sink slowly once the weight has touched bottom

Below: A leger with a short trail. This is useful for anchoring buoyant baits such as crust just above the bottom

places where direct casts are impossible. Fish usually hide away under cover of the waving fronds of streamer weed, and the only way to present a bait to them is to allow the leger tackle to roll under with the force of the current.

Legering in lakes

Legering in lakes poses different problems to those encountered in a river. The most obvious difference is that there is no flow to keep the line taut between rod and leger. Some lakes have a thick layer of weed covering the bottom into which leger tackle would simply disappear. I much prefer float tackle for catching fish close to the bank in a lake as it offers the most sensitive way of detecting bites. For fishing at long range for species such as roach and bream, a swing tip is the most effective way of detecting bites.

Larger species such as carp and tench require somewhat different tactics. A dough bobbin indicator will work quite efficiently for tench and, in some instances, for carp but when using large paste baits for carp the resulting runs made by the fish when they pick up a bait require a lot of line to be allowed to run from the spool. Alternatively, after casting out, place the rod on two rests and tighten up the line. Open the bale arm of the reel and draw line down to the ground. Fold a piece of silver paper over the line but do not trap it completely. As a carp picks up the bait and begins to run, the line will draw through the rod rings flicking

Improvised bobbin indicators for legering can be made from silver paper (1) or even a small twig (2).

A fixed spool reel with the bale arm open to allow line to run off freely

on the end of a line using no additional weight. This is a method for catching the larger species of fish because the bait has to be heavy enough to be cast without additional weight. In lakes it is an effective way of catching tench and carp. Bites are easily detected by watching the point where the line enters the water. As a fish picks up the bait the line will start twitching and then the bow in the line between the rod and the water will begin to lift and tighten.

In a river freelining can be a deadly way of catching chub, especially in the shallows. A large knob of cheesepaste or a big wad of bread flake moulded round the hook will often be grabbed so violently as it trundles along with the current that the rod is nearly pulled from your grasp.

A slight variation of freelining is to use floating baits for fish feeding on the surface. The classic example of this is using a floating crust to catch carp in a lake. A piece of breadcrust is fastened on to the hook and cast out on to the surface of the lake. This is a very exciting method of fishing, especially when you notice a large carp slowly circling round below your bait. It is tempting to strike too soon when you actually see the carp open its mouth and suck in your breadcrust. Control your strike until the fish turns and your line pulls across the surface. Having pulled hooks straight out of the mouths of several carp by striking too eagerly, I speak with experience on this point.

the silver paper clear. The line is then free to run from the spool offering little resistance to the fish. When you decide to strike, lift the rod clear of the rests, close the bale arm and, as the line tightens, drive the hook home. Anglers who specialize in carp fishing have devised many complicated and ingenious methods for detecting bites but the beginner will catch plenty of fish without these refinements.

Freelining

Strictly speaking freelining is not really legering, but because it is normally employed using a leger rod and does not involve the use of a float, I have included it in this chapter. Freelining, as the name suggests, is simply a method of presenting the fish with a baited hook

Carp will frequently circle a floating crust bait before accepting it. This is a good bait to use in summer when carp feed at the surface

Rod tip legering

At one time this was the standard method for detecting bites whilst legering. After casting out, the line was tightened up and the rod was propped at an angle against a rod rest. Bites were detected by watching for any movement of the rod tip. For the larger species of fish this is still a successful method of legering but the smaller species require the more delicate addition of a fine quiver tip. A good quiver tip is also a big improvement when trying for the larger species although you should catch plenty of fish without one.

Bites can vary a great deal from continuous tweaks and rattles to a full-blooded lunging of the rod. When legering in a heavy current the force of the flow will cause the rod tip to bend over. A bite is frequently signalled by the rod tip springing back before lunging down again.

Legering can never be as delicate as float fishing, but used correctly it is a skilful and enjoyable method.

Baits for fishing

Anticipation is part of the enjoyment of fishing, and the preparation of baits for a day's fishing greatly enhances this anticipation. Some baits can be conveniently bought over a shop counter whilst others have to be collected.

Maggots

Without doubt the most convenient bait, and the most widely used by anglers, is the maggot. The commercial liver maggot can be readily bought from most fishing tackle shops. Maggots are sold by the pint measure (0·57 litre) and can be used to tempt most species of fish. Some shops sell the maggots in sawdust or dry groundbait whilst others sell them without an absorption agent, and these are known as solids.

Maggots can be kept quite easily, providing a few simple precautions are taken. Keep the maggots in a plastic container and ensure that the air holes in the lid are kept clear. Never over-fill the bait container, and in the summer months it is advisable to only half-fill it with maggots. If you buy solids then they will keep a lot better if dry groundbait or bran is added. Always try to store your maggots in a cool place before fishing. Maggots are always a lot more active in warm weather and the friction of them all wriggling and rubbing together makes them secrete

ammonia. Kept in a container with no air circulation and no absorption agent, maggots will simply 'sweat' causing them to froth up and smell. As well as making them unpleasant to handle, sweating maggots quickly die and are useless as bait.

In the summer it is advisable to buy only enough maggots for the day's fishing. During the winter months maggots can be kept in a bait container for a lot longer without coming to any harm, although the skins will become more leathery than the skins of fresh maggots. In very cold weather this can be an advantage. Low water temperatures cause fresh, soft-skinned maggots to elongate and become lifeless in the water, whereas the old, tougher-skinned maggots still retain a bit of life.

Maggots in a plastic bait box

Pinkies are the larvae of the greenbottle fly and squatts are the larvae of the housefly. Pinkies are smaller than the liver maggot and squatts are smaller still. Both pinkies and squatts are used mainly for match fishing and are best ignored by the beginner. The amount of maggots needed for a day's fishing depends a great deal on the kind of water being fished. For most situations the beginner will catch plenty of fish with a pint of maggots. In winter, when fish are a lot less active, a pint of maggots may well be enough for several fishing trips.

How to use maggots

For use as bait, the maggots should be hooked through the skin at the blunt end. The hook should be very sharp and the point should be just pushed through the skin of the maggot near the two 'eyes' at the rear end. Care should be taken not to burst the maggot whilst it is being impaled on the hook. Correctly hooked maggots are free to wriggle which increases their attractiveness to fish. Maggots can be fished either singly or in bunches depending on the species of fish you are trying to catch. One or two maggots can be fished on a size 16 or 18 hook whereas a size 6 or 8 hook would need to be used for a bunch of a dozen maggots.

Maggots can also be fed into the swim as loose feed to encourage fish to feed. On some heavily fished waters anglers have introduced so many maggots into the water over the years that the fish have come to accept them as part of their natural diet. Some species, notably barbel, have become so used to maggots on these waters that it is often difficult to get them to accept a different bait. The main drawback with using maggots is that they are a totally

Maggots and casters can be used singly or in bunches

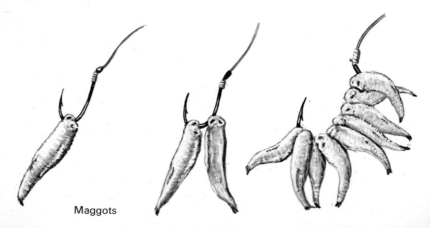

Maggots

unselective bait. On the majority of waters small fish greatly outnumber the larger ones and the angler wishing to catch decent sized fish is best advised to use a larger bait which the little fish cannot tackle.

Casters

Maggot chrysalises are called casters, and they are an excellent bait for most species of fish. Like maggots, casters can be bought from a good tackle shop and are sold by the pint (0·57 litre) measure. As soon as maggots start to pupate the chrysalises are lifted out and placed in a cold storage area. By storing the chrysalises in cold temperatures (not freezing) the development of the pupae is halted. If the chrysalis has developed too far then it will float and lose its effectiveness as a bait. Casters cannot be kept very long so should be bought

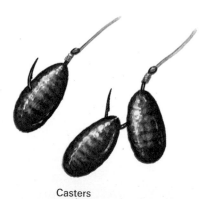

Casters

immediately before the fishing trip, and can then be used singly or in pairs on a fine hook. Sizes 16 and 18 barbless hooks are ideal for caster fishing. The fine, sharp hook should be pushed carefully through one end of the caster's shell. They are easily crushed and care should be taken not to burst the bait as the hook is being inserted. Like maggots, casters are not a very selective bait and can easily be tackled by very small fish, but they are an excellent bait for species such as roach or dace. Loose fed into the water, casters will also encourage fish to feed and will draw them into the vicinity of the hookbait.

Lobworms

Unlike maggots and casters, which are quite expensive, worms are not only an excellent bait but are free. All that is required is a little effort and forethought. Lobworms are the largest worms and are an excellent bait for the larger species of fish such as tench, barbel and chub. Some of the largest roach on record have also been caught on lobworms. Many anglers confuse big garden worms with lobworms, but lobworms are not often encountered whilst digging soil and the only sure way of collecting them is to catch them after dark on damp evenings when they come to the surface of a lawn or flowerbed. The best times of year to collect plenty of lobworms are October and November and then again in March

COLLECTING LOBWORMS
In dry weather water the lawn well or
the worms will stay underground

Above: At night lobworms come to the
surface and can be collected with the aid
of a torch

Below: Store lobworms in a bucket filled
with shredded damp newspaper

and April. The ideal conditions are
very damp, mild evenings with little
or no wind. Hundreds of lobworms
can be collected in a single evening
by creeping across a well mown lawn
and picking them up in the light of a
torch. On really wet evenings lobworms will even surface between the
cracks in paving stones so collecting
them is not very difficult.

Any damaged worms should be
thrown away and the rest can be
stored quite easily for many months
in plastic buckets, provided they are
not overcrowded. Soak sheets of
newspaper in water then squeeze out

the surplus water and shred the paper into a bucket. Fill it nearly to the top with the damp paper and then tip in the lobworms. If they are left overnight the healthy worms will work themselves down amongst the paper and the damaged ones left on top can be thrown away. Store the worms in a cool, well-ventilated spot such as the corner of the garage and you will have a plentiful supply of worms when you want them. The paper can be changed every few months and ideally the top layer should be kept damp. There is no need to feed the lobworms as they eat the paper which is made from plant pulp. If you add tea leaves or compost this will quickly kill these worms since decomposition of the material will produce heat which they cannot tolerate. If you store lobworms this way you will have plenty of bait in summer when long daylight hours and dry conditions make collecting them impossible.

How to use lobworms

A lobworm should be fished by passing the hook just once through the head end of the worm. There is absolutely no need to pass the hook two or three times through the worm so that the bait ends up looking like a big granny knot. A chub or tench can suck the largest lobworm into its mouth faster than you can see. The size of hook depends on the size of the worm but it should be large – a size 4 to size 10. For the average sized roach a lobworm's tail fished on a size 12 hook is a good bait. In flood conditions lobworms take some beating as a bait and even dace will tackle a huge lobworm.

Damaged worms remain on top and should be removed. Keep the paper damp at all times

A lobworm correctly hooked

Redworms, brandlings and other worms

Redworms and brandlings are excellent baits but they are not quite so easy to obtain as lobworms. *Redworms*, sometimes called cockspur, thrive in compost heaps and unless you know a keen gardener locally the only way to ensure a ready supply is to create a small compost heap in your garden. *Brandlings* can also be found in compost heaps but they thrive better in manure heaps and unless you live near a farm you are unlikely to find an easy supply. Another type of worm to be found on the fringe of a compost heap is the *gilt tail*. This tiny worm is red at the head and has a yellowish tip to its tail. Unlike most worms it is rather stiff and does not wriggle but it is excellent bait for grayling and trout. Redworms, brandlings and gilt tails should be fished on a hook size 10 to 16 depending on the size of the worm.

The ordinary garden worms encountered whilst digging will all catch fish but are not as effective as the ones I have mentioned.

Redworm on hook

1.

2.

3.

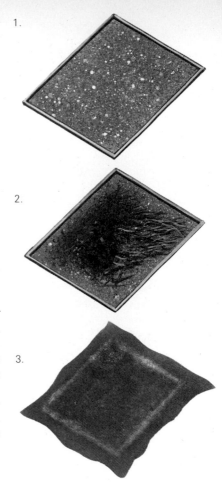

MAKING A WORMERY
1. Dig a patch of earth, clearing any stones or twigs. Mark the area with sticks
2. Mix old tea leaves, grass and vegetable scraps in with the soil
3. Keep the patch wet and dark by covering it with sacking. Lots of earthworms will move into the wormery and provide a source of bait

Bread

A loaf of bread can provide three excellent baits for fishing. The inside of a fresh loaf can be used as flake, the crust can be cut into squares and used as chub or carp bait, and an old loaf can be used to make bread paste. For bread flake all you need is a fresh, white, unsliced loaf. Simply break open the loaf and gently squeeze some of the soft inside bread round the shank of the hook so that the fluffy part is around the hook point. The size of the bait and the hook depends on the type of fish you are trying to catch. For chub or carp you can use a really large wad of flake on a size 4 hook; for roach and dace use a tiny piece on a size 16 hook.

Bread crust is probably the most effective chub bait, especially in winter. A loaf a couple of days old is the best to use for crust. If the loaf is too fresh then the crust is very soft; too old and the crust dries out and

Soft bread flake pinched on to the hook

crumbles when you try to pass the hook through it. To remove a chunk of crust for the hook, insert the point of a knife into the side of the loaf and cut a square with the blade. The crust can then be removed with a portion of flake attached to it. If you examine the crust carefully you will notice that it has a grain rather like wood. Pass the hook through one edge of the crust so that it comes out at the flake side. Ensure that the hook enters the crust at right angles to the grain and not parallel to it. Failure to do this may allow the bait to fly off the hook when casting. Take the

hook through the crust, under the flake, and penetrate the opposite side of the square with the point. If you then gently hold the crust and pull the line, the crust will curl round and the soft flake will envelop the hook. Fastened this way the hook will be hidden from the fish and the crust will not be shaken off by the clumsiest of casting. The size of hook depends on the size of bait you want to use. A size 8 hook is about right for a piece of crust one inch square (2.5 centimetres square).

Bread paste is made by adding water to stale bread and kneading with the hands. The correct consistency is achieved when the paste is soft enough to mould with the fingers but is not sticky. If you accidentally add too much water then put the paste into a muslin bag and squeeze out the surplus water. Pull off a piece of paste the desired size and mould it round the hook.

DIFFERENT TYPES OF BREAD BAITS

Bread crust

Bread flake

Bread paste

MAKING GROUNDBAIT FROM OLD BREAD

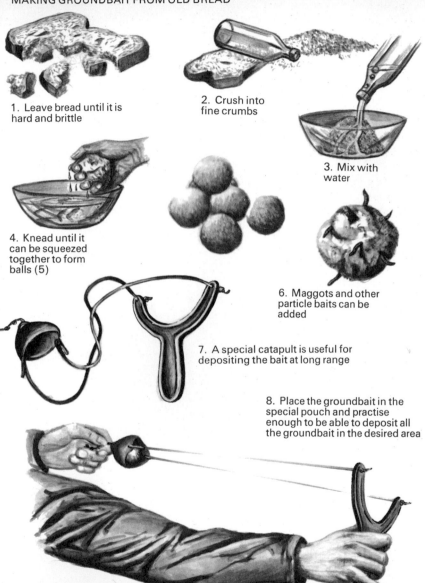

1. Leave bread until it is hard and brittle

2. Crush into fine crumbs

3. Mix with water

4. Knead until it can be squeezed together to form balls (5)

6. Maggots and other particle baits can be added

7. A special catapult is useful for depositing the bait at long range

8. Place the groundbait in the special pouch and practise enough to be able to deposit all the groundbait in the desired area

Cheese

Cheese paste is a good bait for chub and barbel but in some waters it is also an excellent bait for roach. All types of cheese will catch fish but the most adaptable for fishing is the soft, rubbery, processed cheese. All that you need to do with this type of cheese is to mould a piece round the hook. The drier, more crumbly, cheeses need to be worked into bread paste to make them more pliable.

Sweetcorn

In recent years sweetcorn has proved to be one of the best carp baits. Often referred to as particle bait, sweetcorn is not only an excellent carp bait but equally effective for tench, roach and, on some waters, barbel. Sweetcorn can be bought frozen or in tins. The juice which is found with tinned sweetcorn is an additional attraction for fish if added to groundbait. The grains of sweetcorn can be fished singly or in bunches depending on the species of fish you are trying to catch. Medium sized roach can be caught easily on sweetcorn but the grains of corn are too large for the really small fish to manage. Tins of corn are best opened at home and the bait carried in a plastic bait container. This avoids the possibility of cutting your hands on the sharp edges of the tin at the waterside, or your leaving the tin where some animal may find it and injure itself.

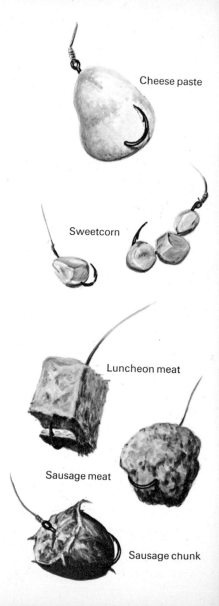

Cheese paste

Sweetcorn

Luncheon meat

Sausage meat

Sausage chunk

Meat baits

Meat baits catch plenty of chub, barbel and carp. Luncheon meat should be cut into bait-sized cubes, and if any problem is found with the meat flying off when casting, a tiny piece of bread can be fixed behind the hook point to secure the meat in position. Like sweetcorn, the luncheon meat is best removed from the tin at home and the bait taken to the waterside in a plastic bait container. Discarded tin cans have become a serious problem on some waters in recent years.

Sausage meat is widely used as a barbel bait but it will also catch plenty of chub. The sausage meat can be bought loose and mixed with bread paste to bind it together, or else sausage portions can be used raw or partly cooked.

Seed baits

Seed baits are good baits in summer for roach, tench, carp and chub, but because a certain amount of effort is needed to prepare them they are not as widely used as they deserve. The main seed baits are wheat, hemp and tares. All these seed baits can be bought unprepared from good tackle shops.

Wheat

To prepare wheat for use it should first be washed in cold water to remove any loose husks. It should then be placed in a bowl, boiling water poured over it and then left to soak overnight. The wheat is then ready to be placed in a saucepan, water added and then gently brought to the boil. The wheat swells enormously and it is ready as soon as the grains begin to split. It should finally be rinsed in cold water and stored in a clean bait tin. This may seem a complicated procedure but it is really only a case of wash the wheat; soak; boil; and then wash again.

Hemp

The preparation of hemp is similar to that of wheat. The hemp is washed and then put in a pan of water. A teaspoonful of bicarbonate of soda should be added to darken the grains. The water is then brought to the boil and allowed to simmer until the seeds begin to split. As soon as this happens the hemp must be removed from the pan and rinsed in cold water.

Tares

The preparation of tares, better known as pigeon peas, is slightly more complicated. The aim with tares is to cook them without the outer skins splitting. After washing in cold water the tares should be placed in a pan and boiling water poured over them. They should be left to soak in this pan overnight. Once again bicarbonate of soda can be added with a teaspoon to darken the seed. No more than one teaspoonful should be used as too much bicarbonate of soda will cause the tares to burst. Place the pan on the stove after soaking and bring the water to the boil. As soon as the water begins to boil reduce the heat so that the tares gently simmer. Cooking tares takes about 10 minutes and they need to be watched all the time. When properly cooked the outer skin should be unbroken but the seed is soft enough to be squeezed flat under finger pressure. Allow the cooked tares to cool slowly and do not wash under the cold tap as with hemp and wheat. Wheat, hemp and tares should be kept moist in the bait tins and not allowed to dry out.

HOW TO PREPARE WHEAT AND HEMP

1. Soak the seeds in water

2. Bring the water to the boil and simmer gently

Wheat

Hemp

Tares

3. Wash with cold water

One important point with the preparation of these seed baits is that the pans used should be old ones which are no longer used for cooking family meals because they are likely to become stained with the seed juices.

In winter all seed baits lose their effectiveness so are best used in the summer and autumn.

Natural baits

The list of baits which will catch fish is nearly endless but those I have mentioned in detail form the bulk of successful baits. The beginner to fishing will probably restrict his baits to maggots, worms and bread. As you become a little more experienced at fishing, do not limit yourself to just a few baits but experiment with different hook samples. Far too many anglers limit their bait to maggots and, by doing so, severely restrict their chances of catching lots of good fish. There are a lot of natural baits which catch fish but a supply is not always available or else they cannot be collected in any quantity. Some natural baits are wasp grubs, caddis fly larvae, stone fly larvae (creepers), slugs, swan mussels, woodlice, crayfish, brook lamprey and elderberries.

Always take at least three different baits with you on a fishing trip so that if one fails you can give the fish a change of menu.

NATURAL BAITS

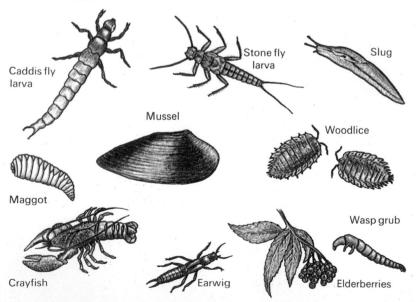

Caddis fly larva

Stone fly larva

Slug

Mussel

Woodlice

Maggot

Crayfish

Earwig

Wasp grub

Elderberries

Fishing for predators

A slightly more unorthodox style of fishing has to be used to catch predators. All fish are predatory to a certain extent, especially just after spawning. Some fish, such as pike, zander and perch, are confirmed predators. Other species such as chub, trout and eels are far more predatory than many anglers appreciate. All these fish will fall to fish baits, used dead or alive, and spin-ning, but you have to choose your tackle to suit those predators with sharp teeth and those without. Pike and zander should be treated dif-ferently to the other predators. The reasons for dealing with these two predators separately is that precautions have to be taken to prevent these fish biting through the line and the fact that they grow very much larger than the other species.

A hooked pike fights hard and will often leap clear of the surface

Deadbaiting for pike

The tackle used for pike fishing needs to be very strong. Not only must the tackle subdue a large and powerful fish, but it must also withstand the exertions of casting heavy baits. Some anglers use a carp rod for pike fishing and this is fine if you are only casting small fish baits moderate distances. If you need to fish at long range with larger fish baits then a more powerful rod is needed. The line should also be strong, especially if you are fishing in areas where there are snags or where large pike are likely to be encountered. Lines between 10 lb and 15 lb (4·5 kg and 6·75 kg) breaking strain are not too heavy.

Bait fish for deadbaiting

Just about any species of fish will catch pike, but some are more effective than others and, equally important, are more easily obtained. One of the most effective deadbaits I have used are sprats. These small sea fish are cheap to buy from your local fishmonger and, being very silvery, are great pike attracters. Sprats are about the same size as large bleak, and 2 lb (0·9 kg) of sprats will be enough for a couple of days pike fishing. Sprats are seasonal fish and unfortunately there may be times when they are unobtainable from your fishmonger. When buying sprats always try to buy fresh ones because deep frozen sprats tend to go very soft and mushy when thawed out. This makes them difficult to

keep on the hooks. Other sea fish which make good deadbaits are herrings and mackerel. These are more expensive than sprats but both these baits have accounted for some very big pike. Herrings and mackerel can be used whole, or cut in two and half the fish used as bait.

The best deadbaits amongst European freshwater species are roach, dace, small chub and gudgeon. Perch and ruffe will also catch pike but their green colouration makes them less visible, and therefore poor

DEADBAIT MOUNTINGS

Sprat on a single hook

Half herring on two treble hooks

baits for static deadbaiting. Worked through the water using sink and draw tactics (see overleaf) these species will attract plenty of pike. One of the most effective deadbaits is a small grayling, but this species is very limited in distribution and only a minority of anglers have access to a grayling river. If your family owns a deep freeze your deadbaits can be obtained in the summer months when they are easier to catch and stored for use during the autumn and winter months.

The size of the bait fish you retain for pike fishing depends on the type of pike water you fish regularly. Some anglers claim that the larger your bait the larger the pike you are likely to catch. This does not necessarily follow and I have caught several pike larger than 20 lb (9 kg) when using a sprat deadbait. As a rough guide I would be more likely to use a large deadbait such as a herring when trying to catch pike at long range in a big reservoir or gravel pit, and use a sprat with the sink and draw method when searching for pike in a weedy river.

Sink and draw deadbaiting

This is the simplest method of deadbaiting, and it is very effective. Some anglers mistakenly believe that deadbaiting is a static and inactive method of fishing. This is not so, for this technique of deadbaiting can be a very active and absorbing method of catching pike. Use a wire trace when pike fishing to prevent the sharp teeth of the pike from severing the

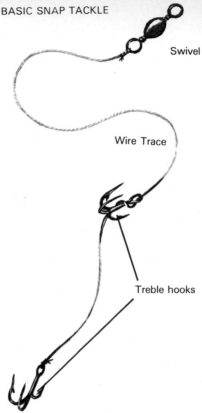

BASIC SNAP TACKLE

Swivel

Wire Trace

Treble hooks

reel line. Lengths of wire trace can be bought separately from most good tackle shops or else they can be bought already attached to two treble hooks. Lengths of wire trace complete with treble hooks are known as *snap tackle*. Wire to be used for traces when pike fishing should be supple as well as strong. If the wire is not very flexible the bait will not be presented to the pike in a natural manner and is likely to be rejected or ignored.

The length of the wire trace should not be much less than half a metre. When using small fish baits such as roach or gudgeon use a single treble hook fastened to the end of the trace, or a large single hook. A swivel should be fastened to the other end of the wire trace to which the reel line can be tied using a clinch knot. The number of treble hooks you fasten to the trace or the decision to use one large single hook depends largely upon the size and shape of the bait fish you use. Pike have very hard bony mouths into which you have to secure a firm hookhold when you strike. A pike will grab a fish bait across the middle before turning it to swallow it head first. If you use a large deadbait two, or even three, treble hooks will ensure a better chance of hooking your pike whilst it is holding the fish crosswise in its jaws. A small bait fish such as a roach or gudgeon will be engulfed in the pike's jaws immediately, so one treble or a large single hook will give you a good chance of hooking the pike.

USING A SNAP SWIVEL

Open catch

Attached to eye of spinner

For repeatedly casting and retrieving a deadbait it is best to use a small to medium sized bait. Repeated casting with a large bait will strain your tackle and cause a great deal of disturbance to the water. Always ensure that the swim bladder of the bait fish is punctured before using it or it will float. This can be achieved by sticking a baiting needle into the body at intervals along the fish.

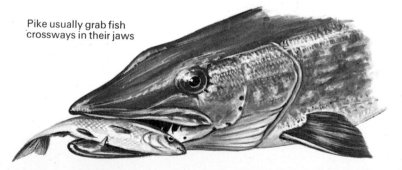

Pike usually grab fish crossways in their jaws

Sprats are a fairly soft bait so, to prevent them falling off the hook during casting, mount them on two small treble hooks set a few centimetres apart. Stick the point of the end treble into the mouth of the sprat and a point of the second treble into the back of the sprat near the dorsal fin. Gudgeon and small roach can be mounted in similar fashion or by simply hooking the mouth of the bait fish with a single barb.

No leads or floats are necessary for fishing with the sink and draw method. The bait fish is cast out into the swim and allowed to flutter enticingly down through the water.

Very often a pike will grab the bait as it sinks through the water. If no bites are forthcoming allow the bait to remain on the bottom a minute or two, then raise the rod tip and reel in a few turns to lift the bait up through

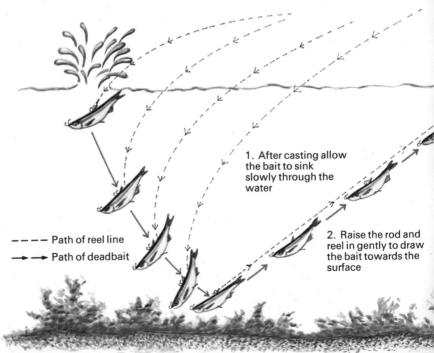

— — — Path of reel line
→ → Path of deadbait

1. After casting allow the bait to sink slowly through the water

2. Raise the rod and reel in gently to draw the bait towards the surface

the water. Repeat this process until you eventually draw the bait into the bank again. The idea is to keep the bait constantly fluttering up from the bottom and then sinking again to imitate a sick fish. Few pike can resist

a bait worked this way, and if pike are in the vicinity one will soon make its presence known. The pike will attack the bait in several different ways. Some fish will lunge at the bait as it is sinking and move off quickly. Others will approach the bait whilst it is resting on the bottom and grab hold as soon as you lift the rod to move the bait. Some pike will gently pick up the stationary bait giving no indication of their having done so until you lift the rod to retrieve and feel the heavy pressure. Do not delay the strike when using small baits fished sink and draw. To ensure you drive the hooks home properly,

Sprat deadbait mounted for sink and draw on two treble hooks, one in the mouth and one near the dorsal fin

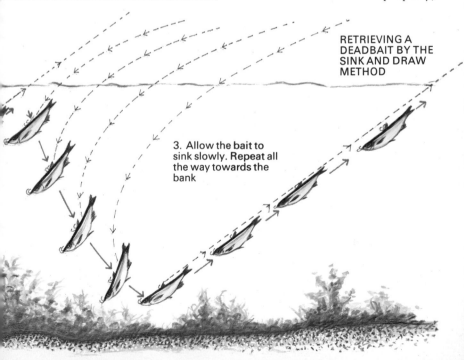

RETRIEVING A DEADBAIT BY THE SINK AND DRAW METHOD

3. Allow the bait to sink slowly. Repeat all the way towards the bank

tighten up the line and sweep the rod back in a smooth but powerful strike. The emphasis is on a smooth strike rather than a hasty snatch.

By fishing a deadbait by the sink and draw method you can cover many likely looking swims. If no bites occur after half a dozen retrieves, then move to another spot and try again. This is a very active method of catching pike and you can cover as much water as you can livebaiting. It is also just as successful.

Static deadbaiting

As the name suggests this method of fishing for pike is something of a waiting game. Pike are confirmed scavengers and will readily pick up a dead fish which is lying on the bottom. The deadbait can be fished using freelining tactics or, if you want to cast small fish baits long distances, a running leger can be added to assist casting. When using large sea fish baits such as herring or mackerel mount them on two treble hooks. Hook one treble in the gill flap of the bait and the other in the back near the dorsal fin. When casting long distances it is often wise to bind the trace to the body of the fish with thread to withstand the force of casting. After casting out reel in the slack line and place the rod on two rod rests. The back rest should be higher than the front one so that the rod is inclined towards the water. In windy weather it is best to sink the rod tip under the surface to avoid wind interference. Leave the bale arm of the reel open so that a pike can pick up the bait and move away without feeling any undue resistance.

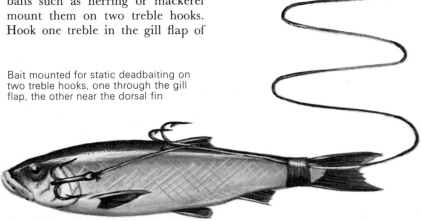

Bait mounted for static deadbaiting on two treble hooks, one through the gill flap, the other near the dorsal fin

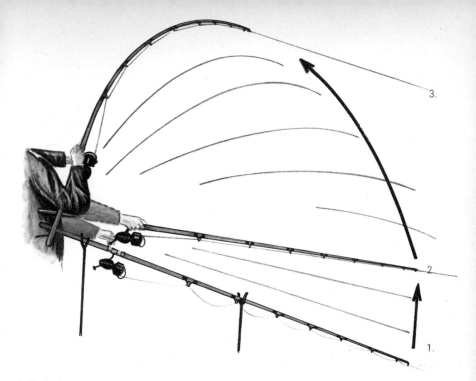

1. Rod placed on rests with tip inclined towards the water
2. Rod pointing at the surface of the water

3. To strike bring the rod back smoothly but hard enough to set the hooks

A bobbin indicator can be used next to the reel to indicate a bite. This need not be sophisticated; silver paper folded across the line is quite effective. When you notice a pike pulling line off the reel, remove the silver paper and pick up the rod, leaving the reel bale arm open. When you decide to strike, close the bale arm and wait until the moving pike takes up the tension on the line, and then sweep the rod back smoothly. When you are fishing at very long range begin the strike by pointing the rod tip at the water so that the

rod travels in a big arc before the strike is completed. This compensates for any stretch in the nylon line which may cushion the strike and prevent the hooks from penetrating the pike's bony jaws.

Floatfished deadbaits

Deadbaits can also be fished effectively by suspending them below a float. Do not use the large traditional pike bung, but use a streamlined float sufficiently buoyant to support the weight of the bait fish and yet large enough to be seen easily. A float can be used to indicate takes from a pike

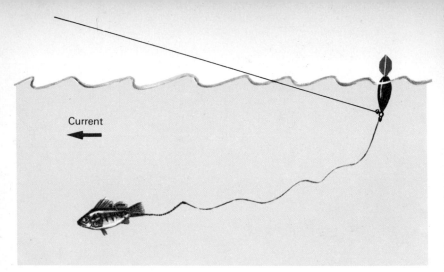

Current

when fishing on the bottom, or to support a bait fished in midwater. On a large lake a float can be used to drift a deadbait across a large area of water. This is an effective way of searching for pike in a lake during windy weather. The surface drift carries the float across the lake and tows the deadbait along after it. If you have the deadbait well clear of the bottom the float bobbing up and down in the waves transmits this movement to the deadbait which will attract the pike.

Another effective method of presenting a deadbait is by using a paternoster rig. The bait is anchored in position with a lead on the bottom and the fish is suspended at the required depth. This is an effective method for presenting a bait above weedbeds. For this method it is better to use a dead fish which has not had its swim bladder punctured, and so floats clear of the line.

Above: Deadbaits can be effectively fished using float tackle and allowed to drift with the wind

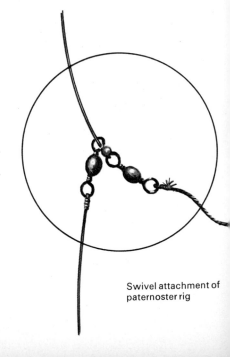

Swivel attachment of paternoster rig

A paternoster rig suspends the bait clear of weedbeds

Lead weight on bottom to anchor bait

A whole mackerel deadbait for pike to be used in conjunction with a float. A modern, streamlined float is used

Preparing to unhook a pike. The artery forceps ensure that your fingers are kept well away from the sharp teeth

Livebaiting for pike

This is the oldest method for catching pike. A live fish is mounted on hooks and cast out into likely looking pike areas. The struggles of the bait fish attract the pike which then surges in to attack the bait. Livebaiting is an effective method for catching pike but it is one of the few methods of fishing which can justifiably be alleged to be cruel.

The methods of presenting a livebait are very similar to those employed in deadbaiting. The simplest way is to mount the livebait on two treble hooks attached to a wire trace and suspend this below a streamlined pike float. Livebaits can also be presented on paternoster and leger tackle.

Pike are scavengers and will just as readily accept a deadbait presented correctly as they will a livebait. Deadbaits can be worked in such a way as to imitate the struggles of a sick or injured fish. By spinning and deadbaiting the angler has ample scope to catch plenty of pike without ever having to resort to livebaiting.

Fishing for zander

The methods used for catching zander are very similar to those used for catching pike but the strength of the tackle has to be somewhat reduced. Zander do not have the huge mouth of a pike and are not capable of dealing with big fish baits. When a zander grabs a small fish it will often swim a considerable distance before attempting to swallow it, so the smaller the fish bait the greater your chance of hooking the zander. Small rudd and roach up to 4 inches (10 cm) long are good zander baits. Gudgeon are also good zander baits and they have the advantage over other small fish baits in that the flesh is firmer, allowing a more secure hookhold. This is an advantage when having to cast the bait long distances to reach feeding zander. When live-baiting for zander with float tackle use the smallest and most stream-lined float that will support your bait – zander are likely to drop your bait if they feel any excessive resistance. A reel line of 6 lb (2.75 kg) breaking

strain is strong enough to land most zander. Use a fine elasticum wire trace because it is more than likely when zander fishing that a number of pike will be caught. Mount your bait on two size 10 treble hooks as for pike. Deadbaits can be presented for zander on standard leger tackle using an Arlesey bomb.

Deadbaiting for eels

Deadbaiting for eels can be great fun, especially after dark during summer and autumn. In a lake the deadbait can be freelined when fishing reasonably close to the bank. When fishing at long range or in a flowing river, straightforward leger tackle can be used. Eels are not tackle shy, so make sure your line is strong. A 10 lb line (4.5 kg) should be enough

STANDARD LIVE BAIT RIG FOR PIKE

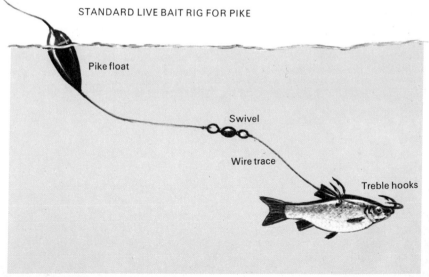

Pike float

Swivel

Wire trace

Treble hooks

to land eels in all but the most obstacle strewn stretches of water. Eels have small teeth, and it is highly unlikely that they will chew through the nylon, so a wire trace is not required. The best way of mounting a deadbait for eels is by using a baiting needle. With the baiting needle pass the line through the vent of the deadbait and out through the mouth. Tie on a large single hook and pull on the line so that the hook bend comes to rest against the mouth of the deadbait. To prevent the deadbait sliding back along the line, pinch a big split shot on the line near to the vent of the deadbait. Small roach, rudd, bleak and gudgeon make the best deadbaits for eels. Whenever possible leave the bale arm open on your reel so that when an eel picks up your bait

it can draw line from the reel before you strike. In a strong flowing river this is not possible so, as soon as you notice the tell tale knocks on the rod end, pick up your rod and release a little line by hand.

Chub and perch

Both these species will fall to the same method of using small fish as baits. No wire trace is needed as these fish are not capable of biting through your line. Chub have very powerful crushing teeth in their throats but you should have struck into the fish long before your bait is swallowed. Livebaits should be small and lip-hooked with a large single hook. Minnows, bleak, gudgeon and bull-heads are all good baits for perch and

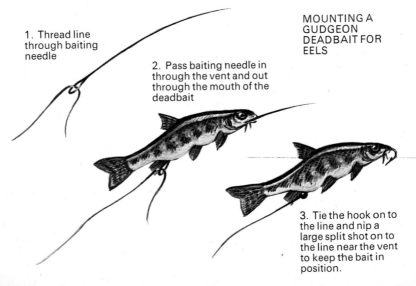

1. Thread line through baiting needle

2. Pass baiting needle in through the vent and out through the mouth of the deadbait

MOUNTING A GUDGEON DEADBAIT FOR EELS

3. Tie the hook on to the line and nip a large split shot on to the line near the vent to keep the bait in position.

chub. Large streamlined avon floats will support most small livebaits but failing this try a small bob float. Unless you are fishing in really deep water no extra weight is needed and the livebait will work better without split shot on the line. Experiment with fishing the bait at different depths. Perch will often be chasing fry between midwater and the surface during the summer months. When chub fishing, unless you are using a really large gudgeon as bait, strike shortly after the float has disappeared. Chub have large cavernous mouths and will begin to swallow the bait immediately. Give perch a little longer as they will frequently run with the bait before swallowing it, and so striking too quickly will lose the fish.

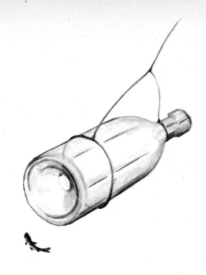

A minnow trap made from a wine bottle. Placed in shallow water with bits of bread inside it, minnows swim in through the narrow neck and cannot find the way out again

Below: A minnow lip-hooked for tempting chub and perch

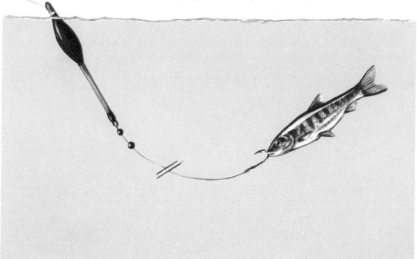

A collection of spinners, plugs and spoons

Spinning

It is possible to catch all the predators except eels by spinning for them. This is a mobile method of fishing for predators and with a spinner you can search a lot of water. The size and shape of the spinner should be chosen to suit the species of fish you wish to catch. Small mepps and Devon minnows will catch plenty of zander, perch and chub. For pike use large mepps or kidney spoons. Special short rods are sold for spinning but a 10 foot (3 metre) carp or barbel rod works equally well. To prevent your line kinking as the spinner revolves, tie at least one swivel into your line a short distance away from the spinner. The spinners themselves are attached to a swivel but this is often in-

Above: Two perch taken on a spinner

Spinning for pike alongside a reedbed

Above: A selection of spinners

adequate for preventing line kinking. When spinning always try to vary the speed of retrieval. Reel in a series of quick turns and then slow down. This way the spinner will lift and fall through the water in a very enticing way. Do not reel in too quickly, and do not lift the spinner out until it is right up to the bank – fish will often follow the spinner right up to the edge of the water and grab it at the last moment.

Plugs are used very successfully for pike in weedy water. Plug fishing is similar to spinning except that the plug dives and wobbles instead of revolving. On the front of the plug is a spoon-shaped vane. This causes the plug to dive as it is being reeled in. The faster you reel then the deeper the plug will dive and can look exactly like an injured fish.

Fly-fishing

Fly-fishing was once regarded (and still is by some people) as a superior method of catching fish. The skills of fly-fishing were greatly exaggerated, causing many anglers to be dissuaded from even attempting this method of fishing. Another reason which deterred anglers from attempting fly-fishing is that it is mainly used to catch trout and grayling, and the number of available waters with these species were limited. In recent years, however, there has been a great upsurge in the popularity of trout fly-fishing and hundreds of new waters have been made available for this branch of the sport. Large supply reservoirs have been stocked with trout and opened up for day ticket fishing, and numerous small lakes have been created and stocked with trout. More people than ever before now have the opportunity to fly-fish for trout.

This angler is fully equipped for a day's fly-fishing without being overburdened

A large rainbow trout in superb condition

Fly-fishing is a skilful method of catching fish and a very enjoyable one. It is no more difficult to master than any other form of angling, however.

Basically there are two main branches of fly-fishing. In one instance the artificial fly is presented to the fish in such a way as to represent an insect which forms part of the fish's natural food. The other form of fly-fishing (sometimes referred to as lure-fishing) is to present an artificial lure to a trout as an imitation of a small fish; sometimes it is worked through the water in such a way as to trigger off the predatory instinct of the fish so that it grabs at the lure as it passes its nose.

Rods and reels

Whichever form of fly-fishing you undertake, the most important thing is to select a rod, reel and fly line that balance correctly. Not only will this enable you to cast with ease but will save wear and tear on the tackle and possible breakages. Rods and fly lines are marked with a number so that they can be matched. The rods can range from A.F.T.M.3 to A.F.T.M. 12. This mark is printed on the rod next to the handle. A.F.T.M. simply stands for Association of Fishing Tackle Makers and it is the number which is important. The lower the number then the lighter and more delicate the rod. An A.F.T.M.3 rated rod would be used for delicate river and stream fishing whilst an A.F.T.M.12 rod is used for casting out a heavy salmon line. For general river fishing and light reservoir fishing, rods in the A.F.T.M.5 to 7 range are ideal. Some rods are designed to use one particular size of line whilst others will cope with a range of line

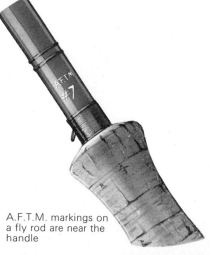

A.F.T.M. markings on a fly rod are near the handle

sizes. For general fly-fishing on a river I would recommend a rod with the range A.F.T.M.5 to 6.

For the beginner a glass fibre rod with a springy action is probably the best to use as it will stand up to the strain of learning to cast. The length of the rod depends a lot on personal

A young boy should be able to cast with an 8½ foot (2·6 metres) fly rod

build. A rod of between 8 and 8½ feet (2·4 to 2·6 metres) is about right for a youngster of 10 to 12 years old. The range of rods is so extensive that it is a good idea for the beginner to take along an experienced fly angler as an adviser if possible when choosing the rod. Take your time over choosing a fly rod and handle as many as you like to get the feel of them. If you are buying a reel at the same time, fit the reel on to the rod and check the balance of the outfit. Don't choose a reel which is too heavy and don't be tempted to buy an automatic fly reel to learn with. As a general rule, the shorter the rod then the lighter the reel you should choose.

Fly-lines

Fly-lines can be very expensive and the beginner should buy one of the cheaper varieties to use when learning to cast. An expensive fly-line can crack and split easily with clumsy casting so it is wise to learn to cast with a cheap line. The size of line should be chosen to suit the A.F.T.M. rating of the rod. Several types of fly-line are available and the novice should make sure he is buying the right one. For delicate presentation of fly and for most general use there is the double taper fly-line. As the name suggests these lines are thickest in the centre and taper gradually to each end. These are denoted by the letters D.T. before the size number. Weight-forward lines are self explanatory and are used where distance casting is more important than delicate presentation, although they can be cast delicately with practice. These are denoted by the letters w.f. before the size number. Floating fly-lines are denoted by the letter f. after the size number, and sinking lines by the letter s. The most versatile line for the beginner to choose for an A.F.T.M.6 rod would be a d.t.6f. fly line.

Fly-lines look thick and clumsy but it must be remembered that it is the weight of the fly-line which carries the artificial fly to the fish. One of the advantages of using a double taper fly-line for river or small lake fishing is that, since it is rare to cast more than half the fly-line when fishing, if one half begins to show signs of wear and tear, the line can simply be reversed and so two fly-lines are bought for the price of one. Fly-lines are usually only 30 yards (27 metres) long and need some backing wound on to the reel beneath the fly-line. It is unlikely that you will ever hook a fish large enough to strip all the fly-line off the reel, especially in a river, but it is always wise to be prepared. Braided backing line can be purchased from a tackle shop and should be securely fastened on to the end of the fly-line. A length of tapered nylon called a leader is attached to the hook end of the fly-line. It is this nylon leader which actually presents the fly to the fish, and leaders are sold in three yard lengths (2·7 metres) size coded from o x to 6 x.

This code denotes the diameter at the tip of the leader and the corresponding breaking strain. As an example, o x leaders have a breaking strain of 10 lb (4·5 kg) and size 6 x leaders have a breaking strain of 2 lb (0·9 kg). The higher the number, the finer the leader point. The leader

Leader attached by a figure-of-eight knot to the hook end of the fly line. A length of nylon line fastened to the leader by a blood knot joins on to the fly

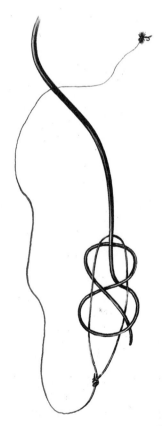

tapers gradually from the loop which joins on to the fly-line down to the fine point. A short length of nylon line of the same breaking strain as the leader tip should be tied to the end of the leader with a blood knot. This length of nylon should be about 18 inches (0·46 metres) long and is known as the point. The idea of having a nylon point on the end of the leader is that every time you change a fly you are reducing the length of nylon line. If you tied the flies direct to the nylon leader you would be working back along the tapered length. After having used several flies you would have worked back along the tapered line so far that the point breaking strain would increase considerably, causing clumsy fly presentation.

Three turn blood knot for attaching nylon line to leader

Figure-of-eight knot

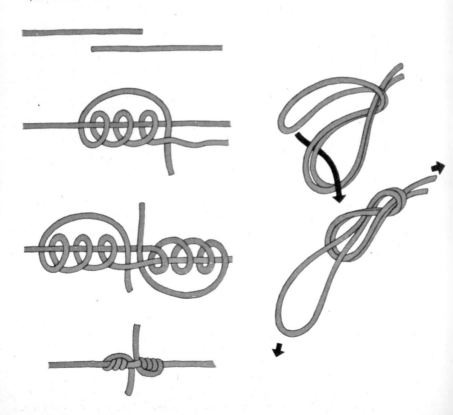

Casting a fly into the teeth of a strong wind on a reservoir

Casting

The problem of learning to cast with fly tackle is the most difficult part of fly-fishing and in reality cannot be mastered by reading about it. The secret is that you must not be deterred from trying, because casting a fly-line is not nearly as difficult as it looks. To begin with you should aim at a delicate presentation and not be too bothered about casting long distances. Take your tackle to an open space and practise casting the fly-line. Don't attach a fly or even the

nylon leader. It is the fly-line you are casting and not the fly.

Pull off several metres of fly-line and lay it along the ground. Hold the rod handle lightly but firmly in your hand with your thumb along the top of the handle. Keep your elbow tucked in against your side so that you use only your forearm and wrist to power the rod. Before starting to cast, the rod tip should be slightly tilted up from the horizontal position. Raise the rod smoothly in an upward arc and, without pausing, power it back when you reach the 10 o'clock position until you reach a 12 o'clock position and the rod is vertical. In this position pause whilst the fly-line begins to straighten out behind the rod. As it does so the rod tip will bend back beyond the vertical position. Just before the fly-line straightens out completely behind you, power the rod forward towards the 10 o'clock position and then,

again without pausing, let the rod drift down to a near horizontal position. This will propel the line forward, and if you have cast it correctly the line will land across the ground in a straight line. No amount of written instruction can compare with actual practice where you can get the feel of the tackle and see the results of your actions.

FLY CASTING TECHNIQUE

1. Begin to steadily lift the rod

2. At the 10 o'clock position power the rod back without pausing until it is vertical

Feather tied to a hook with the barb cut off. This can be used for safely practising casting

The correct hand grip for fly casting

Once you have mastered this step you should try the same process with the tapered nylon leader attached. The next step is to try false casting where, once you have completed the forward power stroke at 10 o'clock, you pause instead of following through, and as the line begins to straighten out in front of you, power the rod into the back stroke. It is by false casting that you lengthen your cast as you keep the fly-line in the air. Pull off a short length of line from the reel with your spare hand and release it at the end of the forward stroke. Don't be impatient when learning to cast, but take satisfaction from each improvement you make. Being able to master your tackle is part of the enjoyment of fishing.

3. Pause whilst the line straightens out behind you

4. Power the rod forward to the 10 o'clock position

5. Without pausing allow the rod to drift down as the line alights on the water

6. Final position of rod after cast is complete

Dry fly-fishing

One of the most enjoyable aspects of fly-fishing is that you can wander along the side of a river without being weighted down with a lot of tackle. All you need is a box of flies and a few sundry items in a small haversack. You can carry your rod and landing net. Dry fly-fishing is to my mind one of the nicest ways of catching fish. The nylon leader should be greased with silicone line grease to make it float, and whatever pattern of dry fly you choose should be dipped in silicone fly floatant. Let the liquid dry for about a minute before casting and the fly will float for a long time.

Dry fly-fishing is normally practised by casting upstream and across so that as the line drifts back towards you with the current, line can be drawn in with the spare hand so you keep in contact with the fly. Let the line you draw back fall at your feet so that when you recast you can let it shoot out again, and do not have to start pulling it off the reel. When you see a fish rising, try to get reasonably close to it without scaring it. Cast up and across to the fish so that as the fly passes into the vision of the fish it isn't preceded by the line. Try to remember when casting to a fish that they are facing upstream into the current. Cast about a metre in front of the fish rather than directly on to its nose end. When trout are stationed just under the surface the rise is likely to be a very gentle one as the fish sucks the fly under. Never be in too

Pheasant tail

Spider fly

Buzzer nymph

Dandy nymph

Escort

Gladiator

Grayling this big are rare

Trotting a fast glide for grayling

much of a hurry to drive the hook home and try to straighten up rather than strike hard. Just hold the loose fly-line with one hand and raise the rod with the other. To strike hard will almost inevitably break the nylon point.

Grayling are fish which can be very difficult to hook at times. This problem arises because grayling have underslung mouths and have to rise in a vertical position to take the fly and then roll over. It pays to watch for the nylon leader to move foward when dry fly-fishing for grayling.

Wet fly-fishing

Wet fly-fishing calls for slightly different tactics. The object of fishing a wet fly is to imitate a drowned insect or the nymph stage of

PARTS OF A FLY

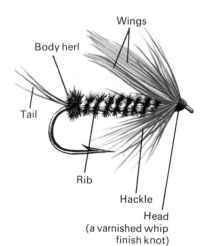

Wings

Body herl

Tail

Rib

Hackle

Head
(a varnished whip
finish knot)

SELECTION OF DRY FLIES

Hook has turned up eye

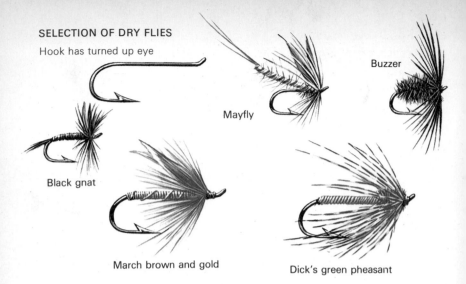

Buzzer

Mayfly

Black gnat

March brown and gold

Dick's green pheasant

a fly which lives under water. In most instances a fly can be fished wet, still using a floating fly-line. The nylon leader is 3 yards (2·7 metres) long and if this is rubbed with a ball of fuller's earth wetted with washing up liquid it will be de-greased and sink. This length will get a fly down to the bottom of most rivers, lots of small lakes and the margins of reservoirs. In a river a wet fly is cast across the current and allowed to swing down with the flow. Once the line has straightened out, immediately downstream from where you are positioned, the line can be gently drawn back. The bites from a fish during wet fly-fishing can be sudden and violent so it is advisable to use a slightly stronger leader than when dry fly-fishing. In fast water the fish grabs the fly so viciously that it often succeeds in hooking itself.

The advantage of having a floating line for this type of fishing is that you can watch the point where the leader enters the water, and if you get a gentle take whilst the fly is moving down in the current the line will pull across the surface. When fishing small lakes the fly is cast out and the leader is allowed to sink. Very often it is whilst it is sinking that a trout will grab the fly. Once the fly has sunk it can be moved gently back towards the bank by drawing on the fly line. A fish taking the fly will move the line across the surface.

The type of fly you use depends a great deal on the state of the river and the time of year. If an easily identified species of fly, on which the fish are feeding, is hatching then it is common sense to use a pattern which imitates this insect. A general way of identifying whether an artificial fly

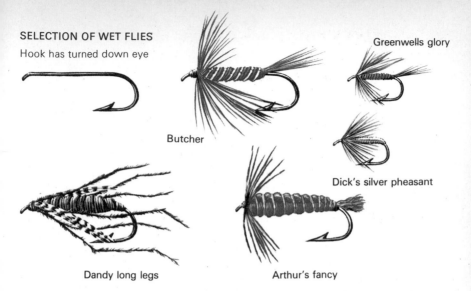

SELECTION OF WET FLIES

Hook has turned down eye

Butcher

Greenwells glory

Dick's silver pheasant

Dandy long legs

Arthur's fancy

should be fished wet or dry is that the eye on the wet fly hook turns down towards the point and on a dry fly hook they turn up away from the point. Look after the flies you use and don't keep dry flies in boxes with hook clips. Stored like this the delicate dry fly hackles will become damaged. A tip for restoring the hackles in dry flies if they do get squashed is to hold the hook with a pair of long tweezers and pass the fly across the steam from the spout of a boiling kettle. All the hackles will spring back to their original position, but take care not to burn your fingers whilst doing it.

Lure-fishing

Lure-fishing is practised on lakes and big reservoirs and requires much stronger tackle since the conditions encountered on a reservoir are sometimes rough. On a large, open expanse of water the wind can whip the waves up to resemble an inland sea. The rod has to be powerful enough to punch a fly line out into the wind. Anglers wading in the margins disturb the fish so that on well fished reservoirs long casting from the bank is occasionally a necessity. The rod should be in the range A.F.T.M.7 to A.F.T.M.9 with a line size to match. For lure-fishing the beginner should use a weight forward line and one which sinks to get the lure down to the fish. The nylon leader should also be a lot stronger than for ordinary fly fishing.

The actual lures are tied to long shank hooks and in the hand look quite pretty but unlike anything you find in the water. It is the movement through the water, given to lures by

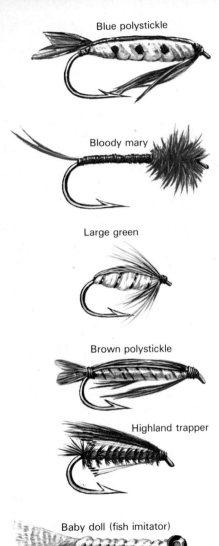

Blue polystickle

Bloody mary

Large green

Brown polystickle

Highland trapper

Baby doll (fish imitator)

reeling in the line, which attracts the trout. The feathers and wool which form the lure are chosen for the colour patterns which, when moved underwater, resemble the colour features of a small fish. The line should be cast out into the reservoir and given plenty of time to sink. Keeping the rod tip pointing slightly down towards the water, strip back the line to work the lure in towards you. Sometimes fish only react when the lure is stripped back at speed and at other times a very slow irregular retrieval will bring results. Do not be in a hurry to lift the lure out of the water for recasting because trout will frequently follow a lure right to the edge before grabbing hold of it.

Playing fish on fly tackle

Opinions differ on how to actually play a fish on fly tackle. One way is to give and take line with the spare hand rather than actually use the reel. Sometimes you must play fish this way especially if a fish takes the lure at your feet when you have just completed retrieving a twenty metre cast. If the fish is large enough it will run out the coils of fly line at your feet, but if not you may have problems getting all the line back into your reel to play the fish in the normal way. Wherever possible I prefer to play the fish on the reel rather than hand play the fish with the fly line.

Lure-fishing, although widely practised on reservoirs, is far from the

The growing popularity of trout fishing is evident from this picture taken on a reservoir on the first day of the season. After the opening day rush the banks are less crowded

only way of catching reservoir trout. Plenty of trout are caught each year using imitation flies fished wet and also with floating lines and flies fished in the surface film.

Fly-tying

Flies are an expensive item in fly-fishing and are easily lost or dam-

aged. It often seems that the more expensive a fly you use the more likely you are to cast into a tree or snap the fly off on the back cast! It is worth the effort for anyone seriously interested in fly-fishing to start tying their own flies. There is a lot of satisfaction in tying a fly and then catching a fish on it. The basic tools you need to begin tying flies are a fly vice; a pair of small and a pair of medium hackle pliers; a dubbing needle; tweezers; and a pair of sharp nosed scissors. Fly-tying materials can be collected on fishing trips. Heron feathers, pheasant tail feathers and pieces of sheep's wool stuck to barbed wire fences can be found

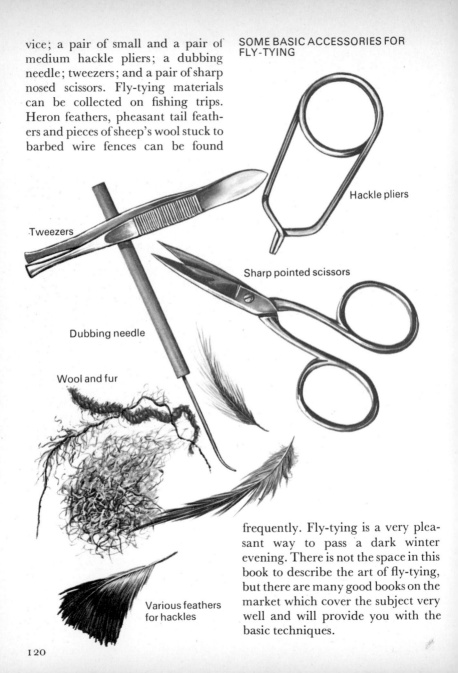

SOME BASIC ACCESSORIES FOR FLY-TYING

Hackle pliers

Tweezers

Sharp pointed scissors

Dubbing needle

Wool and fur

Various feathers for hackles

frequently. Fly-tying is a very pleasant way to pass a dark winter evening. There is not the space in this book to describe the art of fly-tying, but there are many good books on the market which cover the subject very well and will provide you with the basic techniques.

Fly-fishing for coarse fish

Trout and grayling are by no means the only species of fish you catch by fly-fishing. Dace, chub and rudd are great risers to a fly. Chub especially can be interesting to catch on a dry fly during hot weather when they can be seen in shoals just below the surface. Rudd are predominantly surface feeders and fly-fishing for them on a summer evening can produce huge catches. Dace take a dry fly very fast and can be fun to learn on. Perch are regularly caught by anglers fishing with lures on the big reservoirs. Often these perch are of a larger than average size. Pike too will grab a lure as it passes their nose ends. The only problem with hooking pike on fly tackle is that they are likely to bite through the nylon leader.

Fly-fishing can become very absorbing and, once you learn how to do it, a very productive method.

A young angler about to land a big trout from a small 'put and take' trout lake

Rivers

Angling is a very complex subject and to achieve consistent success the angler must learn more than tackle control and the basic habits of fish. He has to learn about the environment in which fish live and how changes in this environment affect fish behaviour.

A river is not just a mass of water draining the land and rushing out to sea, but a very complicated ecological system. Many forms of wildlife are dependent on a river both under the water and along its banks. There are many different types of river from slow, meandering, lowland rivers to torrential mountain streams, each providing a habitat for the different species of fish within them.

Spate rivers

These rivers normally have their beginning, or source, high up in the hills and mountains. They derive their name from the fact that rain very quickly affects their flow; spate being the name for a sudden flood of water. Mountains and hills have more rainfall than the valleys, and consequently the lower reaches of a spate river can suddenly rise and flood when there has been no local rainfall. Because they are subject to sudden rises in level, spate rivers are probably the most difficult of all rivers to fish. The weather therefore plays an important part when fishing

spate rivers – not just the local weather, but the weather in the hills where the river starts.

The tiny trickle of water which forms the beginning of a spate river quickly gains momentum as it flows down the hillside. The bed of the stream is rocky and the water is sometimes stained from peat deposits or iron. Numerous springs and small streams join the main flow so that as soon as the lower slopes of the hills are reached, the size of the river has increased considerably. The river bed will still be boulder strewn but in the deeper pools there will be patches of fine gravel. In these reaches small trout will thrive, keeping under cover of large rocks during the low water levels of summer, and venturing out to feed at dusk and in times of extra water. As the river widens trout become more numerous and grayling appear. The river can vary a great deal in this region, between long shallow glides and narrow rapids. The banks are usually boulder strewn and in hot summer weather the river can be reduced to a trickle between the rocks. Plenty of smaller fish such as bullheads, stone loach and minnows thrive in this region. Crayfish, which look like tiny lobsters, hide away under the rocks. Where they exist, grayling can be found in large numbers and offer good sport right through the winter months.

A spate river during dry weather with exposed gravel beds

After heavy rainfall the river can rise very quickly to form a brown swirling torrent. When fishing the upper reaches of a spate river after recent rain, always be prepared for the river to rise. Take care about crossing on to islands as it is possible for the river to rise before you have time to get back to the bank. In times of spate the fish will congregate in the quieter water near the bank, away from the rushing torrent. Very little weed manages to grow in the upper reaches of a spate river because there is no silt in which the plants can anchor their roots. Insect life is restricted to those species of fly whose larvae or nymphs live under the rocks and stones. The nymphs tend to have flattened bodies so they can withstand the fast flowing water, and are of great importance to the fly angler

The power of this spate river in flood has caused the rock face to collapse

stretches but at spawning time roach will often venture into the shallow, fast water. The nature of the river bed alters, and the gravel is replaced in the slower areas by hard clay or silt. Weed becomes more abundant and the river looks altogether more luxuriant. The river bankings become clearly defined and are often lined with overhanging willow and alder trees. Pike can be found in the deeper pools and although they may not be numerous they can grow very large. The river is still subject to

Right: Shallows in the middle reaches of a river

Below: The upper reaches of a spate river

as they are the main food supply of the trout and grayling.

The first coarse fish to appear along a spate river are dace and chub. Both these species thrive in fast flowing water, especially the dace. Chub become more numerous when the river broadens out into a series of deeper pools. Barbel can also be found as far as the upper reaches of a spate river. The upper limit of barbel is largely governed by the nature of the river bed. Although these fish thrive in fast, well oxygenated water, they prefer a river bed of fine gravel rather than rocks and boulders.

The middle reach of a spate river is a mixture of fast shallows and deeper, willow lined glides. Trout and grayling can still be found in the faster stretches of river, but coarse fish begin to predominate. Roach and perch can be found in the deeper

The slow flowing lower reaches of a river

A banking reinforced to prevent erosion

spates but the effect of heavy rain is not quite so immediate or drastic as it is in the upper reaches. The first signs of an impending rise in level is a layer of dust forming on the surface in the margins. The flow gradually begins to quicken and a few twigs and leaves start floating down. If you notice any of these signs do not leave your tackle unattended or you may return to find the level has risen to swamp your belongings. It is often suggested that a spate river provides the best fishing when the level is rising, but in my experience this is not so. The initial surge of extra water brings down a lot of debris and rubbish which, at times, can make fishing impossible. Once this rubbish has been washed away and the level begins to fall again the fishing will improve, especially if the river has been low for several weeks because of dry weather.

Several minor rivers may flow into the main river so that by the time it reaches the flat plains it has swollen to a considerable width. Over the centuries man has played a major part in altering the lower reaches of spate rivers. Because of serious flooding the banks have been built up to confine rivers to their courses.

Modern drainage schemes have included the removal of bankside bushes so that the flow of the water is not slowed down. Very often these rivers are navigable in the lower reaches and boat traffic can seriously interfere with angling. The regular spates of these rivers carries down a great deal of suspended silt and sand in the water which settles on the bottom once the river slows down. This deposit of silt gradually builds up to reduce the depth, so on navigable waterways it is dredged up to keep the channel deep enough for boats. Because of this depth, any weed is confined largely to the margins of the river.

Thus, a stretch of river which is dredged and where any bankside vegetation has been removed is rather featureless and it is not at all easy to determine the likely fish holding areas. Where they exist, weirpools and rougher water immediately downstream are obvious fish holding areas. Barbel and chub will often live right under the weir sill, below the white water. In summer even bream will venture into the weirpools where the water is fast and turbulent. Trout are seldom encountered in these lower reaches but a few do manage to thrive in the weirpools. Weirpools can be very dangerous places to fish so never take any unnecessary risks to reach a fishing spot. Even when very little

Bank erosion where natural vegetation has been removed to help land drainage

water is flowing over the weir sill, green slime and algae can make it very slippery to venture across in rubber boots. Other obvious fish holding areas are where small rivers or streams join the main river, and during floods fish will congregate in these areas.

Lowland rivers

The levels of lowland rivers do not fluctuate nearly so much as spate rivers. In times of heavy rain they will rise and run coloured and in freak conditions they will occasionally flood. Normally the levels of these rivers are more predictable and consequently the angler is not so

dependent on the prevailing weather conditions for his sport. Lowland rivers flowing through rich agricultural land are normally capable of supporting more life than spate rivers. The different zones of a lowland river are not so readily defined and coarse fish are often present right up to the river source. Even when the infant river is just a trickle of water meandering across a meadow, a wide variety of water plants flourishes. In summer the upper reaches of these rivers can become choked with water weed and marginal rushes. Aquatic life is very rich and the fish in this type of river have plenty of food. In the upper reaches the rivers run clear and,

Above: Weirpools can provide some excellent fishing

Below: A lowland river with man made banks

where they are still narrow, fish spotting is relatively easy. The main species of fish likely to be found in these reaches will be chub, dace, roach and perch. As the river increases in width then shoals of bream will appear. The flow on this type of river can vary a great deal. Some lowland rivers are shallow with a lively current flowing over waving beds of streamer weed, whereas others are very slow moving with thick beds of water lilies.

Frequently these lowland rivers join to form a very large river. These large lowland rivers then resemble the lower reaches of a spate river but without the high flood bankings. Most species of fish will be found in these rivers with the exception of grayling. Trout may be present but are uncommon, and the slower flowing rivers are unlikely to support barbel.

Boat traffic can seriously affect fishing

On the smaller rivers, boat traffic can be a serious problem for the angler and the fishing is sometimes better in the winter months when the number of pleasure craft decreases. In the overgrown, weedy stretches of river there is also more open water to fish when the vegetation dies down in the winter.

Drains

These fall into two categories. Some drains are simply small rivers which have been straightened, widened and dredged, whilst others are completely man-made. They are created to drain water away from flat agricultural land and often have little or no flow. The water levels in the drain are controlled by sluice gates which are opened to allow excess water to run off to sea. The banks of these drains are usually very uniform with little or no cover. The species of fish present are those which prefer slow water, such as bream, tench, roach and perch. Large predators, for example pike and zander, often thrive in these drains. Fish location in a drain is difficult because the fish rove about a great deal. Bream shoals will often move several kilometres along a drain in a few days. Zander shoals tend to follow the small fry about, and the key to zander location is to first find the fry on which they feed.

Canals have straight featureless banks

Chalk streams are fast flowing and extremely rich in plant and animal life. Trout in these rivers grow very large

Canals

Originally constructed to transport cargo by barges, many canals have now fallen into disrepair. Those canals which run through large industrial areas are often used by thoughtless people as tipping grounds for domestic waste. Whilst some canals only support small fish, there are a few which offer good sport for the angler. The main species to be found are roach, perch, tench and bream. Some canals hold countless numbers of gudgeon and a few have recently been stocked with carp.

Chalk streams

Chalk streams are the richest of all the types of river and can provide superb fishing. These rivers are fed by rainwater slowly draining through chalk rock and then rising to the surface again through springs. Most chalk rivers are carefully protected trout fisheries and offer some of the finest dry fly-fishing in the world. The water is usually swift flowing and very clear. The temperature of these rivers does not fall very low even in winter and they are rarely subject to serious flooding. The luxuriant weed growth harbours the nymph stage of many species of fly. Coarse fish do exist in chalk streams and can grow to specimen proportions. Because chalk streams are normally managed as fly-only trout fisheries, coarse fish are treated as a nuisance and netted out to reduce competition with the trout.

Lakes & ponds

Many of the species of fish encountered in rivers will also be found in lakes and ponds. Sometimes the species may have arrived naturally in the lake but in many cases man has introduced them to provide sport. Large lakes can be very daunting places to fish. Confronted with a vast expanse of open water the angler is often at a loss where to begin fishing. Wind can whip up large waves on lakes which then take on the appearance of a miniature sea. Having no real current and no obvious features, locating fish in a large lake can be very difficult – especially for the beginner. Lakes and ponds cover a wide range of different environments for fish. Some are shallow and very rich in life whilst others are deep, rocky and barren. In between these two extremes there is a wealth of fishing to be enjoyed in stillwaters.

Lowland lakes

This description covers a wide range of lakes, many of which have been created by man. Lowland lakes are usually capable of supporting a wide variety of fish. The richness of the water depends on several factors.

The water in large upland lakes is often too acid to provide really good fishing

Farm ponds often provide young anglers with their first experience of catching fish

The most important of these is whether the water is acid or alkaline. This is often referred to in terms of 'soft' or 'hard' water. Most lowland lakes are 'hard' or alkaline waters. Acid or 'soft' waters usually occur on higher ground where the water seeps through peat bogs. Alkaline waters are much the richest and are capable of supporting a wide variety of insect, crustacean and fish life. The richest of all lowland lakes are those where the water percolates through chalk rock before running into the lake. Some lakes are totally enclosed but others are fed by a small stream. A few lakes have been created by damming a small stream or river so that the water has risen and flooded over an area of low lying land.

Plant life is usually abundant in lowland lakes. The bankings and margins will support reeds and rushes, whilst the shallows will contain a number of varieties of soft water weed. Many anglers confuse the tall reedmace with the bulrush. The reedmace is the tall plant which grows in thick clumps and develops a brown cigar-shaped head on the main stem. In winter, when the leaves die away, these stems remain upright and the brown seed head begins to disintegrate, scattering seeds out into the water. Reedmace grow in places where the bottom is soft silt or mud, and can spread in shallow lakes so that they eventually cover a large area. True bulrushes have a single green stem which grows to a height of five or six feet (1·5 or 1·82 metres). The narrow stem develops a tiny flower towards its top. Bulrushes grow best where the bottom of the lake is gravelly. Knowing the difference between these two plants is useful because they indicate a different type of lake bed. Advice that tench feed alongside bulrushes is wasted if you can't tell the difference and spend your time fishing alongside reedmace beds. Both these plants are a helpful indication of depth as

Reedmace thrive where the bed of the lake is soft mud. This plant is often wrongly referred to as the bulrush. (*inset*) The brown cigar shaped seedhead of the reedmace

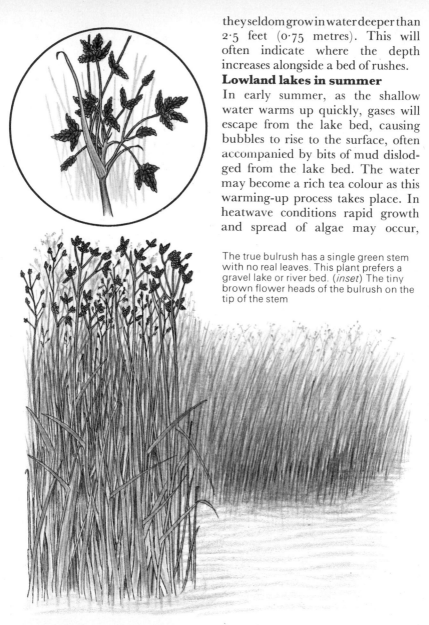

they seldom grow in water deeper than
2·5 feet (0·75 metres). This will
often indicate where the depth
increases alongside a bed of rushes.

Lowland lakes in summer

In early summer, as the shallow
water warms up quickly, gases will
escape from the lake bed, causing
bubbles to rise to the surface, often
accompanied by bits of mud dislodged from the lake bed. The water
may become a rich tea colour as this
warming-up process takes place. In
heatwave conditions rapid growth
and spread of algae may occur,

The true bulrush has a single green stem
with no real leaves. This plant prefers a
gravel lake or river bed. (*inset*) The tiny
brown flower heads of the bulrush on the
tip of the stem

causing the lake to appear green. The surface layer of water warms up very much quicker than the deeper water. In between the layer of warm water and cold water there is a short depth where the temperature changes suddenly. This is called the *thermocline*. In hot, calm weather this thermocline is very noticeable. The surface layer of water will be warm, green and thick with algae and plankton. If you place your arm into the lake you will be able to feel the sudden change in temperature at the thermocline. The plankton and algae

Meres are shallow lakes and can vary in size

SUMMER – CALM CONDITIONS

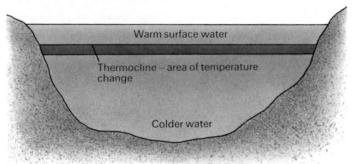

Warm surface water

Thermocline – area of temperature change

Colder water

SUMMER – WINDY CONDITIONS

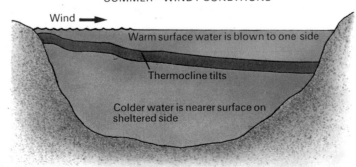

Wind ➡

Warm surface water is blown to one side

Thermocline tilts

Colder water is nearer surface on sheltered side

will be confined to the top layer of warm water so that if you paddle your hand around you will be able to see the clear water below the thermocline. Fish avoid the warm layer of water which contains very little dissolved oxygen. In windy weather the action of the wind will cause the algae and plankton to drift to the windward side of the lake. In these hot weather conditions, it pays to fish with your back to the wind. The thermocline tilts so that the cooler water will rise towards the surface on the sheltered side of the lake and this is where the fish will be. It is easy to tell when there is very little oxygen in the surface layer of a lake during hot weather. Waft a landing net handle around on the surface and it will create large bubbles which are a pale green colour and take a long time to burst. You will also find that your keepnet will not stay extended and keeps folding up and rising to the surface. If you encounter these conditions don't keep your fish in the net or they are likely to die. These conditions are most likely to be encountered in June or early July. In normal summer conditions, when there is no algae or plankton explosion in the lake, the best fishing is likely to be found when casting into the wind. The warm surface layer will contain enough dissolved oxygen for the fish because of the action of the waves. In small lakes the tilting of the thermocline is not nearly so noticeable as it is in larger waters. Water in the shallows will be very warm during the day but cool down slightly at night. Fish often take advantage of this and move into very shallow water to feed after dark.

Lowland lakes in winter

During the colder months of the year, a reversal of this process takes place when the surface layer of water is the coldest. At this time of year fish with your back to the wind as the water layers tilt and the warmer water comes towards the surface on the sheltered side of the lake. Also, it is not much fun trying to fish into the teeth of a January gale! The fish are generally in the deeper parts of the lake.

WINTER

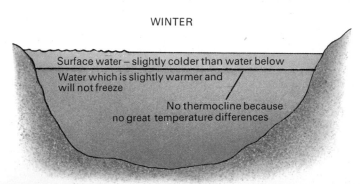

Surface water – slightly colder than water below

Water which is slightly warmer and will not freeze

No thermocline because no great temperature differences

Trees round the margins of a lake can cause problems. When the leaves are shed in the autumn they will eventually become waterlogged and end up on the windward side of the lake. The leaves will form a thick carpet on the lake bed and, as they decompose, they release gases which cause distress to the fish. Avoid these areas during late autumn and winter because you are unlikely to catch many fish.

Locating fish

Locating fish is not very difficult in small lakes. Shoals of rudd and roach often congregate close to the surface where you can see them splashing about. Tench and carp will grub about on the lake bed, frequently discolouring the water and sending masses of bubbles and bits of debris to the surface. Carp will feed amongst the underwater stems of reedmace and bulrush where they eat snails' eggs and small nymphs clinging to the stalks. As the large fish force their way amongst the stems of the rushes, they cause the tops of the rushes above the surface to wave about and in some cases to fold completely over. When carp are seen to be feeding amongst rushes like this, a bait presented along the edge of the rush bed will most likely catch them. Gaps in weedbeds are also good places to fish for most species. Water lily beds always look as though they are good fish-holding areas but they are seldom productive. Carp will venture

amongst the lilies, where they feed on snail eggs on the underside of the pads. The stems of water lilies are extremely tough so, if you fish for carp or tench near these, make sure your tackle is strong. Bream tend to keep to the clear water where they sometimes give away their location by rolling on the surface. When you notice bream rolling it's a safe assumption that they are feeding.

Gravel pits

These are the water-filled lagoons which remain after the land has been quarried for gravel and sand. They vary in size but some of them are very large. Some gravel companies landscape the area when gravel extraction has ceased but other lagoons are left until vegetation appears naturally. The gravel pits are usually stocked with roach, rudd, bream, tench and carp. Few clubs actually stock gravel pits with predators but pike and perch usually find their way in.

Gravel pits are the most difficult of all waters to fish. The main reason for this is because the depth is so uneven. Unless you were fortunate enough to see the workings before they were flooded, it can take many hours fishing to discover the shallow and deep areas. A number of gravel pits are very deep indeed and the deepest areas are seldom very productive. In the deepest water very little insect or crustacean life, on which the fish feed, will thrive. The contours of the

Above: New lakes are being created by digging holes in the ground to extract gravel

Below: Once gravel pits have been landscaped they make attractive and often very productive fisheries for both coarse fish and trout

bed can be roughly determined by looking at the changing colour patterns of the surface. The deeper areas will appear dark blue or green. The water in a gravel pit is usually very clear but in windy conditions the windward side will become coloured as the waves wash in silt from the bankings. The bottom of a gravel pit is usually gravel and hard clay. Some pits are very irregularly shaped with lots of small bays and inlets. Fish location in these areas is easier than in the vast expanses of open water. Try to locate shallow ledges alongside deeper water. Weed will not grow in very deep water, so fish alongside weedbeds. Most lakes are shallowest towards the banks but

A pair of tench caught from a gravel pit

gravel pits sometimes drop away into very deep water close to the bank. Once you find the areas of shallow and deep water, gravel pits can produce some excellent fishing.

Reservoirs

These have been created to provide water for our towns and cities, and are formed by building a massive dam across a steep sided valley so that the land behind the dam is flooded. Because the water is used for supplying domestic needs most water authorities restrict fishing to the use of artificial lures. This means that most reservoirs are run as trout fisheries where the rule is fly-fishing only. They are all artificially stocked with hatchery-reared brown and rainbow trout. The quality of the fishing depends on the management stocking policy, but most provide good trout fishing at a reasonable price. On some reservoirs the stocking takes place on one occasion before the season opens so that the first few weeks of the season produce lots of trout. As the trout are caught, the fishing becomes more difficult towards the end of the season. On other reservoirs the management release trout in batches throughout the season so that the level of sport remains constant. This is often referred to as 'put and take fishing'. Reservoir trout fishing has enabled many more anglers to participate in fly-fishing than would otherwise be possible.

A landscaped lake makes a tranquil setting for early morning tench fishing

Upland lakes and tarns

Most of these waters are poor and unable to support large fish. Many small tarns in mountainous areas are very peaty and brown. Those which are stream fed with plenty of gravelly areas may hold lots of brown trout which seldom grow larger than 8 inches (20 cm) long. Very few coarse fish are likely to be found in this type of water. The only coarse fish which seem able to live in these conditions are perch and pike. The pike may grow to a respectable size, but the perch usually remain small and stunted. In limestone outcrops a few richer lakes can be found which may well produce some very big trout. These richer lakes are easy to distinguish because the water will be very clear with abundant water weed. Fishing in hilly and mountainous areas is very dependent on the weather: even in summer a hill tarn can be a very bleak place to fish.

Fish handling & fishing etiquette

As regular users of the countryside, it is the responsibility of every angler to look after the fishing areas and protect the wildlife. Sadly, a few anglers shirk this responsibility and the behaviour of this minority occasionally results in stretches of water being closed to angling. To carry out these responsibilities requires no effort and quite often it is just a case of common sense and good manners. In no way does a constructive approach to angling detract from the enjoyment of the sport; if anything it greatly enhances the pleasure.

Fish handling

Keepnets
The introduction of knotless keepnets and landing nets has helped a great deal in preventing unnecessary damage to fish. The fins of a fish are very easily split, so, if the fish are to be returned to the water alive, great care should be taken to avoid any damage. The keepnet should be staked out correctly so that the support rings don't fold over and trap the fish. In a flowing river the net should be positioned so that it is parallel with the current and not directly across the flow. Choose a site to place your net where there is sufficient depth to cover the net but where the flow is not too fast: in a fast flow the fish will have to fan their tails to hold position against the current, and tails continually brushing against a keepnet will quickly be worn away. Choose the site for the keepnet before you begin fishing and try to avoid areas where half the keepnet length is out of water because of a steep banking. A fish which

Use a rod rest to keep a big net fully extended in shallow water

Place fish gently into a keepnet. Do not throw them in

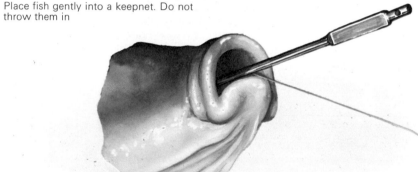

Use a disgorger to remove the hook from a deeply hooked fish

is dropped so that it slithers down a length of dry netting will lose a lot of scales. If the water is swirling in several directions, as frequently happens at the edge of a river, pass a spare rod rest through the bottom end of the net and press it into the riverbed to keep the net extended.

Removing hooks

When you land a fish, try to unhook it as gently and efficiently as possible. Small hooks can be more difficult to remove than large ones, so always have your disgorger handy and use this if you have difficulty grasping the hook with your fingers. Don't pull at the hook but gently ease it out. Barbless hooks are simple to remove even if the fish is hooked in the back of its mouth. With a larger fish it is easier to remove the hook whilst the fish is in the landing net. After unhooking a big fish, grasp it directly behind the gill cover with one hand and support the 'wrist' of the tail with the other hand. Gently place the fish into the keepnet, don't throw it. To return your catch at the end of the day simply lower the mouth of your keepnet, tilt the bottom of the net up slightly, and let the fish swim out. If you want to weigh a particular specimen than place the fish in a polythene shopping bag or a landing net – with the latter method, don't forget to subtract the weight of the net.

Should you want to take a photograph of a fish then make sure your camera equipment is ready before removing the fish from the net. Try to ensure that the fish is out of the water for the minimum time needed to take the photograph. Any fish you want to take home for eating, such as trout or grayling, should be killed quickly and cleanly with a blow to the back of the head with a solid object. Do not kill any more fish than you need.

When you return coarse fish to the water ensure as far as possible they are as healthy as they were when you caught them – keeping your hands wet helps avoid injuries to the fish.

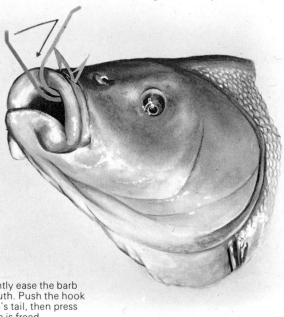

To unhook a fish, gently ease the barb clear of the fish's mouth. Push the hook back towards the fish's tail, then press down so that the barb is freed

Releasing fish by lowering the mouth of the keepnet into the water

When handling a fish try to support its weight, for example against the forearm

Litter

Perhaps the most serious problem to be found on heavily fished stretches of water is litter left behind by thoughtless anglers. It looks unsightly and can kill riverside wildlife. So serious has this problem become in recent years that the Royal Society for the Protection of Birds has carried out a survey which reveals that every

year anglers leave behind many kilometres of discarded nylon line, often with baited hooks attached. It is a slow, agonising death for the robin or songthrush which gobbles up the maggot left on a discarded hook length. Even lengths of nylon left in the grass can tangle round the legs of water birds, trapping them until they starve to death, which may take several days. The sad truth is that

Above: This bird died because an angler left line on the river bank
Below: Litter left by anglers is unsightly and dangerous

these bird deaths and injuries are totally unnecessary since it takes no effort at all to put the offending lengths of nylon into your tackle bag for safe disposal at home. Every angler gets tangles from time to time but, however frustrated or angry you are, never leave nylon fishing line on the riverbank.

Empty tins of sweetcorn or luncheon meat whose contents have been used as bait are nearly as dangerous as discarded lengths of nylon. The jagged edges of the tins can sever the legs of farm animals and badly gash the arm of an unsuspecting angler reaching into the grass. I once saw an oystercatcher flying round with an empty tin of sweetcorn firmly wedged on its leg. One angler

I know was fishing one day when he heard a commotion in the margins a little way upstream. When he walked along to investigate he found that a small chub had its head firmly wedged in an empty tin of corn which some thoughtless angler had thrown into the river. The list of dangerous items of litter is endless, yet the solution is so simple. Do not leave litter of any description on the banking after a day fishing. Even sweet wrappers are unsightly. It is up to the younger generation of anglers to show their elders how to respect the countryside.

Waterside behaviour

The most effective way of making sure you don't catch any fish is to noisily stamp around on the riverbank or lakeside. If you were only spoiling your own chances of catching fish by doing this you would only have yourself to blame, but the chances are that you would be ruining the sport for other anglers fishing nearby or on the opposite bank. Fish are wild creatures and just because they live in a different element to our own doesn't make them any less cautious than other wild animals. Always respect the area being fished by another angler and don't encroach too close without being invited. It is very tempting to start moving closer to an angler who is catching fish from the next swim when you are not getting any bites. There is no harm in politely enquir-

ing from a successful angler what bait and tackle he is using but don't start fishing in his swim. Most anglers will be only too pleased to give tips and information and quite often invite you to fish next to them.

Bankside disturbance is frequently the cause for failing to catch fish so always be careful when walking past other anglers on the river bank. There are times when it is impossible to escape bankside disturbance through no fault of your own. On warm, sunny days many other people besides anglers may be at the waterside. Boaters, picnickers, swimmers and people out for a stroll can all seriously interfere with fishing. On a number of rivers these people have every right to be there so never be rude to them. Instead try to arrange your fishing at the times when the least number of people will be present. Noisy people and boats are not compatible with good fishing, so try and avoid them if you want to catch plenty of fish.

Never interfere with farm livestock or crops growing near the water, and always leave farm gates either open or closed as you found them. If you come across an open gate which should obviously be closed then inform the farmer.

This chapter may appear to be full of do's and don'ts but most of it is just good manners and common sense. It is up to each generation of anglers to look after our fisheries so that other anglers in the future may enjoy the same standard of fishing.

Fish identification

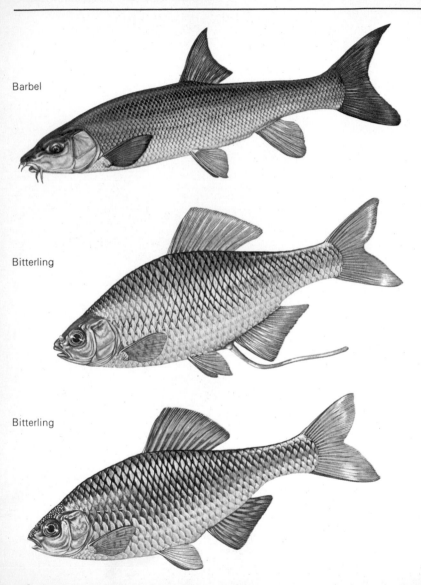

Barbel

Bitterling

Bitterling

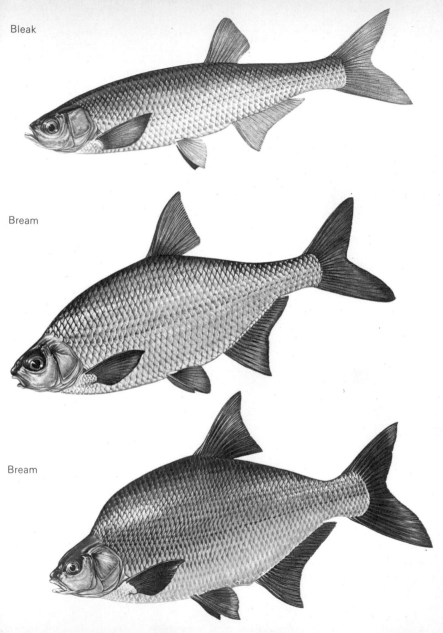

Bleak

Bream

Bream

Carp

Charr

Charr

Brook charr

Chub

Dace

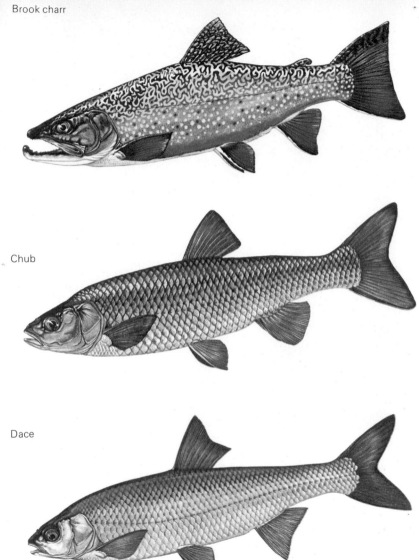

Eel

Grayling

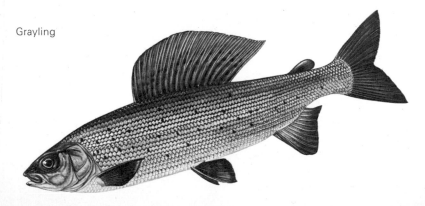

Gudgeon

Minnow

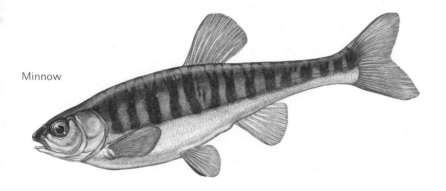

Minnow

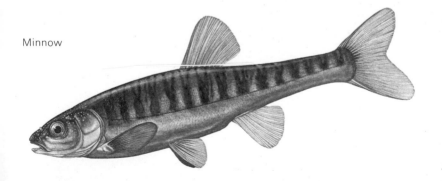

Orfe

Perch

Pike

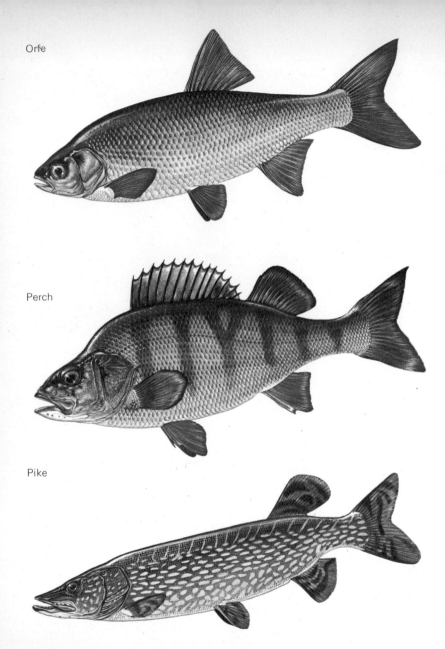

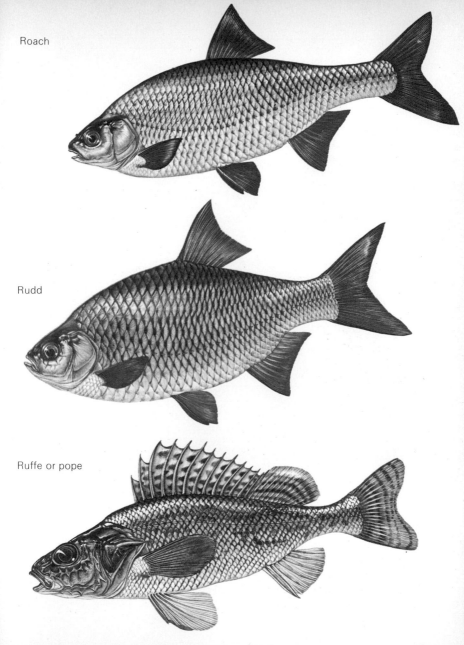

Roach

Rudd

Ruffe or pope

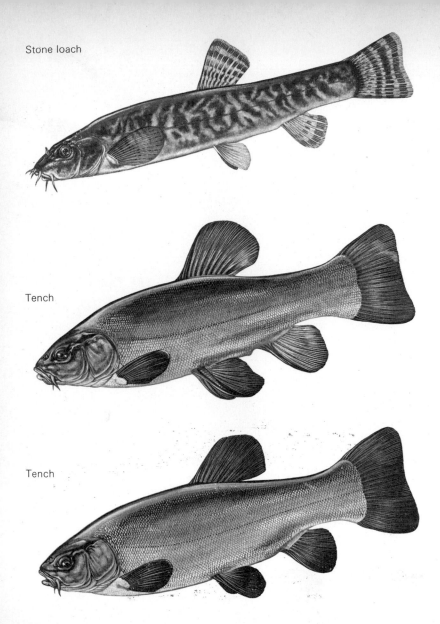

Stone loach

Tench

Tench

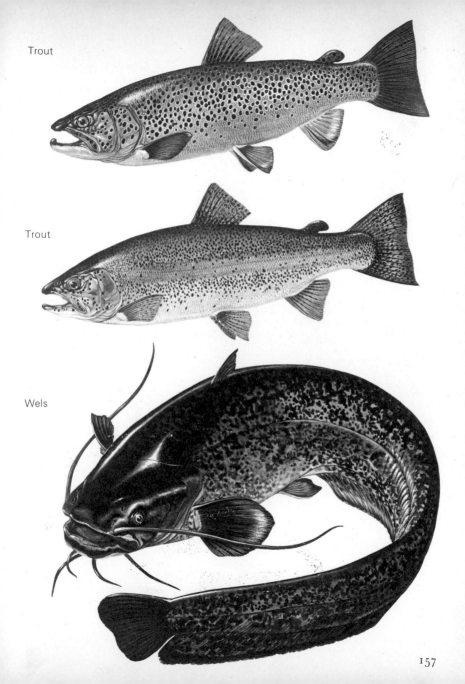

Trout

Trout

Wels

157

Barbel

Barbel are arguably the most powerful fish you are likely to encounter in a river. These fish can grow very large, and in the rivers of Europe may reach a weight of 15 to 20 lb (6·75 to 9 kg). In the rivers of the United Kingdom, the maximum size is slightly less than this. Barbel are perfectly shaped for living in fast flowing rivers where they search for food on the river bed. The barbel has the underslung mouth typical of bottom feeding species, and around it are the four fleshy 'feelers' called barbules from which the fish derives its name. These barbules are used for

A good catch of barbel. Keepnets for retaining this species should be large and knotless

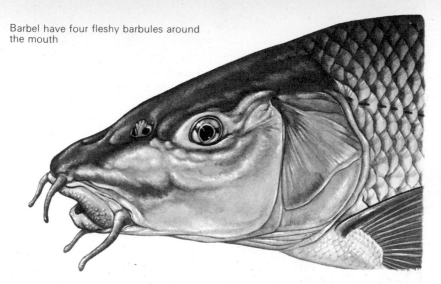

Barbel have four fleshy barbules around the mouth

detecting food at close range. Because of the position of the eyes, the fish is unable to see directly in front of its nose and it detects food by snuffling around in the gravel using these barbules.

Barbel thrive in fast, oxygenated rivers especially those with a gravelly river bed. They will venture into the slower, deeper reaches at times but need shallow, fast water in which to spawn. Barbel are fish of the warmer months of the year and during the winter are less active. They can be caught in the winter during mild spells of weather or when stirred into activity during flood conditions, but serious fishing for them is largely a waste of time. As the water begins to warm up and the daylight hours increase during April, the barbel start moving into the shallows in preparation for spawning. This is the

best time of year to estimate the barbel population on a stretch of river as large numbers of barbel congregate together. Spawning takes place between the middle of May and the middle of June, depending on the prevailing river and weather conditions. Each female fish is escorted by several smaller male fish. The eggs are laid in very fast shallow water where the female creates a depression in the fine gravel or sandy river bed by fanning her tail. Once spawning is completed the barbel spread out along the river. They still form shoals or small groups but not in the same numbers as during spawning time.

Barbel are easiest to catch soon after spawning for two reasons. The first is that for a short while large numbers of barbel are concentrated together and are easy to locate.

3. Amongst streamer weeds
4. The fast water at the head of a pool

LIKELY SPOTS TO HOLD BARBEL
1. Submerged trees and roots
2. Fine gravel or sand

Secondly, barbel tend to feed avidly after spawning to regain their strength. A large shoal of barbel congregated in shallow water is an impressive sight. Individual fish will roll over giving a brief glimpse of their golden sides. This 'flashing' behaviour is very common with barbel and often gives away their location when the water is too deep to see the outline of the fish against the river bed. Flashing is a sign of excitement and so is usually associated with feeding. Barbel which are rolling on to their sides in this manner can usually be caught even if they are not actively digging in the gravel.

Locating barbel

Locating barbel is the key to success because they are seldom evenly dispersed along a stretch of river. In shallow, clear water, barbel can be located easily enough by walking carefully along the banks and spotting the fish. A pair of sunglasses with polarized lenses helps tremendously since they cut out much of the surface glare on the water and allow you to see down to the river bed. On deeper stretches of river where fish spotting is not possible, location becomes more difficult. Sometimes barbel will give away their location by rolling on the surface. They often behave in this way when the river is in spate. I have frequently seen barbel roll on the surface when the river has been swollen by heavy rain and is running very fast and coloured. These are, however, chance sightings and not a reliable way of locating barbel. Locating barbel on a deep featureless stretch of river is often a case of trial and error. Talking to other anglers can be helpful, as can studying fishing match results and pinpointing the spots where any barbel were caught.

On a stretch of river which alternates between fast shallows and deeper pools, barbel can usually be found where the water runs into the head of a pool. Underwater obstructions, such as sunken tree trunks, are also likely barbel-holding areas. The nature of the river bed is also important because barbel prefer fine gravel or sand and tend to avoid the boulder-strewn areas. Where streamer weed is found, barbel will often lie hidden under the trailing fronds, venturing out at dawn and dusk to feed.

Barbel holding areas are not necessarily barbel feeding areas. Unlike some species of fish, barbel do not feed by intercepting particles of food carried down to them by the current. When actively feeding, barbel forage along a defined stretch of river, searching amongst the gravel as they travel upstream. In shallow water the foraging barbel can be seen to leave a stream of discoloured water behind them as they disturb the river bed. On a deep stretch of river it is a common occurrence to catch two or three barbel in rapid succession and then no more. What has happened is that a group of foraging barbel has moved into the area that is being fished and then carried on upstream.

If this happens, try casting upstream to try and locate the foraging shoal of fish. On shallow stretches of river, barbel will venture into very shallow water to feed. Sometimes their backs appear right out of the water as they search about in the margins.

Baits and tackle for catching barbel

Barbel will eat just about anything they disturb from amongst the gravel. Small fish, such as stone loach and bullheads; the nymphs of flies; shrimps; even the algae which covers the gravel in warm weather; all these form the barbels' diet. The strange thing about barbel is that although they will eat almost any organism they find on the river bed, they can be very selective about anglers' baits. On waters which are not heavily fished, it is often difficult to catch barbel with anything but a natural bait, whereas in heavily fished waters, barbel are easier to catch because so much unused bait has been deposited into the river by anglers that barbel have become accustomed to it. On a few rivers so many maggots have been thrown into the water by anglers that barbel are rarely caught on any other bait, and the angler is nearly forced to use maggots for bait. In the case of rivers where there is very little fishing, a natural bait is usually best and the most easily obtainable of these is the lobworm. Other offerings which have proved to be excellent barbel baits are cheese paste, luncheon meat and sausage. On some rivers sweetcorn will also catch a lot of barbel.

Because they are bottom feeders and are usually found in fast flowing rivers, barbel are mostly caught by legering. They are very powerful fish and tackle strong enough to enable you to land them should always be used. A 10 foot carp rod with a through action is ideal. The strength of line depends a great deal on the type of water you are fishing. On open stretches of river a breaking strain of 5 lb (2·25 kg) will be strong enough, but for fishing near sunken branches and snags this should be increased to as much as 10 lb (4·5 kg). Barbel are responsible for more 'lost fish stories' than any other species.

A swan shot link leger is suitable for presenting most baits, but when using maggots a swim feeder is very successful except in extremely shallow water. When barbel are feeding avidly on maggots, they often give false bites by grabbing hold of the swim feeder. Barbel can be caught by float fishing but the bait must be presented on the river bed by fishing over depth. Float fishing works best when the current is not too strong and the river bed is fairly level.

When legering, the bites from barbel can be extremely violent. Never wander off and leave your rod unattended when barbel fishing because if the fish hooks itself when it takes the bait, you may have to save up to buy a new rod. I have seen rods pulled off their rests by barbel.

Barbel are powerful fighters especially when aided by a strong current

The first few runs of a hooked barbel are very powerful and you will have to give line. Even when the fish begins to tire and comes to the surface, be prepared for it to explode into life again and dash away. When you land a barbel treat it very carefully. If you retain the fish in a keepnet, make sure your net is large enough and of a knotless material. The dorsal fin of a barbel has small spines on the first ray and these can become tangled in the net, damaging the fish. In hot weather the fish are best returned immediately to the river.

Above right: Many barbel are lost at the net when they make a last minute bid for freedom

Barbel have a large dorsal fin with tiny spikes on the first ray

Bream

One of the most popular fish with anglers, the bream is widespread throughout Britain and Europe. There are two species of bream, the bronze and the silver. The silver bream is not nearly so common as the bronze bream and does not grow very large. Bronze bream can be large and fish over 12 lb (5·4 kg) have been caught. The small bronze bream are often referred to as skimmers and are generally a silvery colour which closely resembles that of the silver bream. Once the bream have reached about 3 lb (1·4 kg) they take on the darker coloration

The underslung mouth of a sizeable bream

Big catches of shoaling bream can be taken

which gives the species its name. On some waters the bream can be so dark they are nearly black. Bream have deep bodies, but are fairly flat. They are found mainly in lakes and slow flowing rivers, but on some of the larger rivers bream will sometimes shoal in huge numbers in the faster water below a weir. When hooked, bream are not the best of fighters but in flowing water they will use their broad flanks to good advantage. One of the attractions of bream for anglers is that they can often be caught in great numbers. Shoal bream usually weigh between 1 lb and 5 lb (0·45 kg to 2·25 kg). The larger bream are either solitary fish or rove around in small groups.

Locating bream

Bream are bottom feeders and when a massive shoal of fish are feeding madly they can cause the water to become discoloured. This is extremely helpful when trying to locate a shoal of bream. Like barbel, bream have the habit of rolling on or near the surface. At long range you may not actually see the fish, just a series of swirls and a big, black tail appearing above the surface. Bream are also wanderers, and a shoal of fish may travel considerable distances.

Baits and tackle for catching bream

When fishing at close range in a river or lake, an antenna or bodied waggler float should be used and fixed by the bottom end only. Shot the tackle so that the bulk of the weight is immediately below the float and the tackle sinks slowly. Feeding bream will often swim in tiers through the water, and those at the top will accept the bait as it sinks amongst the shoal. Check the length of time it normally takes for that float to cock and settle down in the water. If, after casting out, your tackle doesn't cock in the normal time, strike, because a bream may have taken your bait as it was sinking.

Since the bream are not renowned fighters, your line does not need to be particularly strong. A three pound (1·35 kg) breaking strain line will handle the average shoal bream. In flowing rivers, or when fishing at long range, leger tackle is best employed for bream. This is exactly the situation for which the swing tip bite detector was developed. Cast slightly beyond the feeding fish, and as soon as your tackle lands in the water, reel in quickly to draw your leger into the right spot. Tighten up so that the swing tip is set correctly. Most bream bites are positive and the swing tip will straighten up smoothly. As soon as you have struck into a fish, try and draw it away from the rest of the shoal. When legering for bream it often pays to use a long trail. (The trail is the distance between the hook and the leger weight.) By leaving a long trail the bait will fall slowly to the river or lake bed after the leger weight has landed. Bream will then grab the bait as it is falling. In fairly shallow water, where the activity of the bream is discolouring the water, it is possible to determine the edge of the shoal. Where you can discover this, try and place your hookbait near the fish at the edge of the shoal since fish hooked in the middle of the shoal will eventually scare the remainder with their struggles.

When bream fishing, a common occurrence is for the swing tip to keep twitching up and then falling back. Striking will fail to hook any fish, or occasionally a bream is foul-hooked. The cause of this twitching of the swing tip is bream milling about on the bed of the river or lake and catching your sunken line with their fins. These twitches are often referred to as *line bites*. When you encounter this problem try reeling in a few turns at a time as the bream are milling around between you and your tackle.

Groundbaiting is essential to keep a large shoal of bream feeding in one small area. It is almost impossible to throw in too much groundbait when you discover a large shoal of bream in a wide river during summer. In deep water the groundbait should be moulded into cricket ball sized lumps and lobbed into the feeding area. These balls of groundbait should be firm enough not to break up when they hit the surface. Judging how and when to groundbait for bream is not always easy. A shoal of fish located in shallow water will sometimes move away if large balls of groundbait are crashing into the water above their heads. In this situation small balls of groundbait thrown in at frequent intervals is often the answer.

The most successful baits for bream are worms, maggots, breadpaste, and sweetcorn. Lobworms will catch bream but the tails of lobworms, or redworms, are better. Sometimes a 'cocktail bait' of maggots and a small worm will catch bream when they are finicky. When you catch one bream the chances are that you will catch many more, so do not cram too many into a small keepnet or they will be injured.

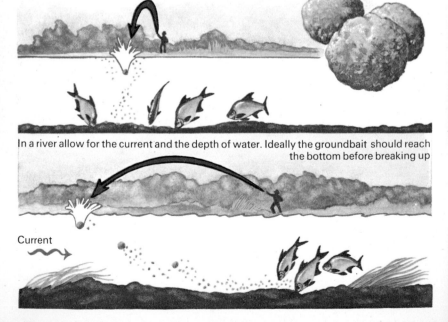

In a lake ensure the groundbait lands in the same spot each time

In a river allow for the current and the depth of water. Ideally the groundbait should reach the bottom before breaking up

Current

Carp

Carp are normally to be found in stillwaters, but they do exist in a number of rivers, including some which are fast flowing. In rivers where the water is used for cooling power stations it is returned to the river very much warmer than when it was taken out, Carp thrive in these warm water conditions below a power station outfall. The best sport with carp is, however, enjoyed in lakes, ponds and gravel pits. Carp are large, heavily built fish and can grow very big in favourable conditions. Most waters are stocked artificially with carp reared in fish farms. The carp species used for stocking lakes is usually the king carp of which there are three main varieties. The mirror carp is only partially scaled and these scales are large and irregularly grouped on the fish's body. The leather carp is virtually scale-less, having a smooth leathery skin. The common carp is perhaps the most handsome, being fully scaled and a beautiful golden-bronze colour. The only species likely to be confused with the king carp varieties are the crucian carp and the wild carp. The crucian carp is a separate species and does not grow very large. It is a much rounder fish and has no barbules around the mouth as does the king carp. The true wild carp is now very rare and is the original carp from which all king carp have been bred. The wild carp is a very lean, fully

The carp's mouth extends telescopically for feeding on the lake bed

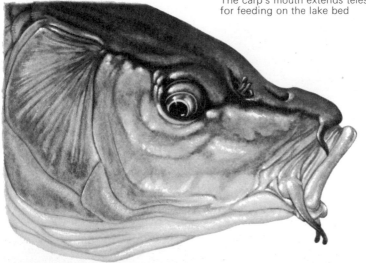

scaled fish and is now so uncommon that few anglers are likely to encounter it.

Carp are fish of the warmer months of the year and, although they do feed during the winter months, trying to catch them then can be a very unrewarding exercise.

Locating carp

Locating carp in a lake is not very difficult. In hot weather they will frequently bask just below the surface. When they are feeding on the lake bed they will disturb lots of silt and discolour the water. If the lake bed is very soft, groups of bubbles will rise to the surface, often accom-

A nice catch of carp taken on sweetcorn

panied by bits of twigs and weed. The most difficult type of water in which to locate carp is a vast gravel pit. Location on this type of water is often a case of trial and error.

Baits and tackle for catching carp

The tackle needed for catching carp must be strong, especially if the water you are fishing is full of lily beds and thick weed. The rod should have a through action and be 10 or 11 feet long (3 or 3·3 metres). Even small carp in open water fight very strongly so the line strength needs to be at least 5 lb (2·25 kg) breaking strain. On really weedy lakes where the carp grow very large, a breaking strain of 12 lb (5·4 kg) is not too heavy.

In recent years, carp fishing has become something of a specialist branch of the sport. Carp are without doubt one of the most difficult species of fish to catch, and, on waters where a lot of fishing for carp takes place, anglers are constantly searching for new baits and tactics. There are still a lot of waters where very little serious fishing is done for carp and on these waters they are not nearly so difficult to tempt. Anglers using maggots to catch small fish are not likely to hook carp, and if they do, the chances are that the carp will break the light tackle being used. When fishing at close range in a lake, a bait can be presented on the bottom using an antenna float to detect bites. At longer range the bait is easier to cast using leger tackle. Most carp waters contain lots of small fish such as roach and rudd so the bait should be chosen and presented in such a way as to avoid the attentions of these fish. Sweetcorn has proved to be one of the best carp baits. Scatter a few grains on the lake bed and then present a couple of grains on a size 8 hook in the centre of these. Sweetcorn is often referred to as a particle bait. Carp do not have to move very far to find another sample when feeding on particle baits, so do not wait long before striking.

If large paste baits are used, carp are more likely to pick up the bait and run with it. Whilst legering or freelining with large paste baits the rod should be mounted on two rod rests. The front rest should be the type which has a deep groove in it to allow the line to run freely and not become trapped under the rod, and should be lower than the back one so that the rod is inclined towards the water. In really windy weather the rod tip should be submerged to cut out wind interference on the line. When using large baits, the bale arm on the reel should be left open so that the fish can take line without feeling any resistance. As the fish begins to run with the bait, lift the rod, close the bale arm and strike as the line tightens up. Bites can be detected by folding silver paper over the line. This will fall clear when you strike

Large carp are strong fighters

Well prepared carp anglers settle down to fish right through the night

into the fish. When legering small particle baits, however, the bale arm should be closed and some form of bobbin indicator fastened on to the line between the first two rod rings. Carp which pick up the bait and don't move away very far cause the bobbin to jerk up and down rapidly. These are often referred to as 'twitchers'.

Carp are quick to associate certain baits with danger and as soon as several of the lake's carp population have been caught on the same bait, they all learn to avoid it. This is why carp anglers are continually experimenting with different baits. The list of carp baits is endless but they will take all sorts of paste baits. The standard ingredient is bread but this can be mixed with cat food, custard powder, sausage meat or cheese. One of the most exciting ways of catching carp is with floating bread crust. A carp will often circle the bread for several minutes before actually taking it.

Carp are very wary and to catch them you cannot afford to create any bankside disturbance. In Britain the largest carp caught weighed 44 lb (19·8 kg) but in Europe they have been reported up to 60 lb (27 kg). Most sport is enjoyed with carp in the 5 lb (2·25 kg) to 10 lb (4·5 kg) size range and any fish over 15 lb (6·75 kg) is a splendid specimen.

Chub

Over the years, chub have gained the reputation of being very shy and suspicious fish. It is perfectly true that chub are not at all tolerant of bankside disturbance but, if a little care is taken when approaching the edge of the river, chub can be very easy to catch. They are greedy fish and will accept most baits readily provided you have taken care not to scare them. Although they have been introduced to a number of lakes, chub are river fish. Chub are widespread throughout the length of the rivers they inhabit, and can often be located in vast shoals. Shoals of chub usually consist of fish weighing between 1½ lb (0·67 kg) and 3½ lb (1·57). As they grow larger the chub tend to become more solitary in their habits, and occasionally grow to over 7 lb (3·2 kg), but in most rivers a 4 pounder (1·8 kg) is a fine fish.

Spawning occurs between the middle of April and the end of May. At spawning time chub develop white tubercles around their head. A chub which has just spawned is in poor condition and not really worth catching. Chub appear to take longer than most other species of fish to completely recover from the effort of spawning. Once they have recovered, they are splendid fish with deep bronze bodies.

Locating chub

Chub like plenty of cover, and thrive in stretches of river where the bankings are lined with overhanging willow bushes. They are not confined to these overgrown stretches, however, and shoals of chub can be found in wide featureless stretches of river.

Chub have large blunt heads

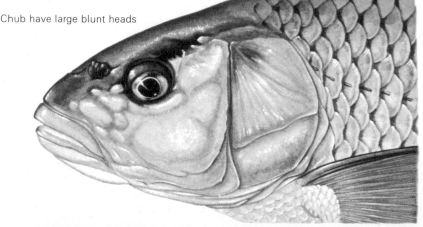

A favourite haunt of big chub is under the overhanging branches of bankside bushes

Baits and tackle for catching chub

Any kind of bait can be used and the fish can be caught right through the year: in some rivers they are the mainstay of sport during the winter months. During the summer, chub will spend a lot of time in the shallows and faster water where they feed on small fish such as stone loach, bullheads, and the fry of coarse fish,

including their own. Freelining cheesepaste in shallow water on a summer evening is one of the most effective methods for catching chub. The hook is tied direct to the line and a knob of cheesepaste is moulded round the hook. There is no need to leave the hook point protruding from the cheese because the force of the strike will pull it clear. The size of the piece of cheese you mould round the hook depends on how far you have to cast, since chub can tackle very large baits. A knob of cheese the size of a pigeon's egg will be heavy enough to cast across most rivers. Cast slightly upstream and hold the rod high to keep as much line clear of the water as possible. Feel for the bites by letting the reel line run over the forefinger of the hand with which you hold the rod. As the cheese trundles along over the river bed, a bite will normally be difficult to miss. The line will zip forward through the water and tighten to the rod. As soon as you have struck, try and draw the chub out of the area so its splashing does not disturb others in the shoal. In the slower reaches freelined cheesepaste works equally well and, by letting your bait trundle along the river bed, you are able to cover a lot of river. Should you want to anchor your bait in a particular spot, simply add a link leger to your line. In hot weather, cheesepaste tends to melt slightly and becomes difficult to cast without it flying off the hook. By adding some breadpaste the bait will become firm enough to stay on the hook.

Bread crust will catch plenty of chub, but during the warmer months it is vulnerable to the attentions of smaller fish. Dace in particular will whittle away at a piece of bread crust and demolish it before the chub have a chance to find it. In winter, when the smaller fish are less active, breadcrust is probably the best chub bait. Crust is buoyant so it has to be firmly anchored to the river bed. This is achieved by stopping the leger weight only one inch (2·5 cm) away from the hook. The leger has to be heavy enough to overcome the buoyancy of the crust, so use an Arlesey bomb, since a link leger is not suitable. As crust softens in the water, it pays to rebait again if no bites are forthcoming after half an hour. In winter, when the water is extremely cold, cheespaste tends to solidify and set like cement around the hook. This makes hook penetration very poor when you strike.

In winter, chub will not be very far away from their summer haunts. In times of flood they may temporarily move out of an area but, generally speaking, a swim which produces lots of chub in summer will still hold plenty of them in winter. In extremely cold water, small baits may catch chub when larger offerings are ignored. Casters have proved to be a good chub bait either legered or float fished. Casters and maggots will catch plenty of chub during the summer, but if hordes of small fish such as bleak and dace are present, the chances are that these will get to

Chub are handsome fish with bronze scales delicately edged in black

the bait first. In winter these small fish are less active, so you can use casters with greater confidence of attracting the chub. Bites from chub in cold weather can be very gentle especially when using a small bait. Even when using crust, chub can pick up the bait giving no more indication than a slight increase of pressure on the line. These are the type of bites which really require touch legering to detect, but in winter, when your hands are likely to

Drifting floating crust down to surface-feeding chub

freeze and long waits between bites are experienced, this method is not really feasible. The best compromise is to use a very sensitive quiver tip and to strike at the slightest tremble or gentle pull.

Chub and barbel can often be caught from the same swim using the same bait and tactics. Unlike barbel, chub are not confirmed bottom feeders and are caught readily using float tackle. In fact, float fished baits often catch more chub than do legered baits. By feeding a steady stream of groundbait into the top of a swim, chub can be encouraged to feed madly. Don't throw in great balls of groundbait when you begin fishing, but feed the swim gradually with small handfuls of groundbait or loose feed. If you suddenly stop getting bites, lower the depth of your float because the fish may well have moved up in the water to intercept the loose feed earlier.

Hot, sunny, windless days in summer are not the best of conditions for catching fish, but chub can still be tempted when all other species refuse to feed. In these conditions chub will often drift around like grey ghosts, just below the surface, occasionally swallowing some unfortunate insect trapped in the surface film. In this situation a piece of floating bread crust can be an excellent bait. Simply fasten the hook into a chunk of bread crust, and using weightless tackle, flick it out a little way upstream from the chub. A few free offerings can be tossed in first to arouse the interest of the fish. No bite detection is needed as you can see the chub grab your bait. In this situation try and strike by keeping your rod tip close to the water and sweeping the rod back in an upstream arc. If you strike vertically the chub will explode into action on the surface and create so much disturbance that it could ruin your chances of catching any more.

Chub have a strong predatory instinct and can be caught using small fish baits or by spinning. This predatory instinct is very strong after spawning, but even during the winter many chub are caught on quite large deadbaits intended for pike. Stone loach and bullheads make excellent chub baits. Bullheads are easy to collect from under rocks in shallow rivers just using your hands. When you lift the rock, they will often lie still on the bottom, allowing you plenty of time to cup your hands round them. Stone loach, however, are very quick off the mark and you need the use of a fine mesh net to catch them. Don't be tempted to use a treble hook when fishing with small fish baits. Pass a large single hook through the lips of the bullhead and trot it down through a likely looking chub pool on float tackle. If chub are present, the float will suddenly disappear without any preliminary bobbing. Strike immediately or else the fish may be deeply hooked.

Bullheads can easily be caught by carefully lifting stones and trapping the fish in cupped hands

Dace

Dace are one of the smaller species of fish and seldom grow larger than 1 lb (0·45 kg). In many rivers, a dace of half this weight is an exceptional fish. Dace thrive in fast flowing rivers but will also be found on some of the slower flowing rivers. During the summer months, vast shoals of dace will congregate where there is a swift flow. Dace will feed anywhere from the river bed to the surface. The beginner may confuse large dace with small chub but once these two species have been compared there are a number of differences. The dace is a more streamlined fish than the chub and has a much smaller head and mouth. The anal and dorsal fins of the dace are concave, whereas those on the chub are convex. An easy way to remember this is to think of the 'curved chub' and the 'dented dace'.

Baits and tackle for catching dace

For their small size, dace are game fighters when using light tackle. A line of 1½ to 2 lb (0·67 to 0·9 kg) breaking strain is ample when dace fishing although an interloping chub may test your skill with this tackle. Maggots and casters are good baits used in conjunction with a size 16 or 18 hook. Being such small fish, dace are not really worth fishing for unless you attempt to catch a lot of them. Feed the swim you are fishing with loose maggots and casters. A small handful

COMPARISON BETWEEN CHUB AND DACE

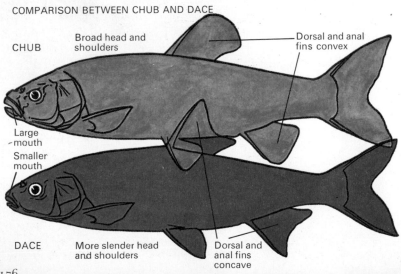

CHUB Broad head and shoulders

Dorsal and anal fins convex

Large mouth

Smaller mouth

DACE More slender head and shoulders

Dorsal and anal fins concave

Trotting for dace in a small river

Catch of dace taken on bronze maggots

thrown in after every few casts will eventually get the fish feeding madly. Begin by fishing slightly over depth but be prepared to lower your float should the dace begin to rise to intercept your loose feed.

On some rivers a spate, following heavy rain, will cause the dace to feed voraciously. In these conditions dace seem prepared to tackle any kind of bait. When the river has been running high and coloured I have frequently caught dace on huge lobworms and size 6 hooks whilst fishing for barbel. This is not the ideal tackle with which to enjoy sport with dace, but I have sometimes taken advantage of finding big shoals of dace by accident and continued to catch them. By scaling down my tackle I have caught most of my larger dace in rivers which were in spate and coloured.

During the winter months dace move away from the heavier currents into the slacker water. Laying on with light float tackle is a good method for catching dace during the winter. By selecting a good swim and carefully feeding loose maggots into the river, you can draw dace in so close that you are catching them under your rod tip. It is not very easy to try and catch the larger dace but do avoid the tiny ones. In many rivers the average dace only weighs a few ounces (grammes) and larger fish than this are rare. In rivers where they exist, big dace tend to keep to the slower water and seldom mix with the shoals of smaller fish.

Dace can be caught on fly tackle and a few hours dry fly-fishing for them can be extremely enjoyable. The rises are very fast, and so must your reactions be to catch them.

Eels

There are very few waters which do not contain eels. The eel is a migratory fish which spawns in the Atlantic Ocean. The tiny eels or elvers drift with the ocean currents to reach Europe in their millions. The elvers find their way up the rivers and streams where they grow to maturity. Eels will travel along the smallest ditch to find their way into

Most of the larger eels, like this massive fish, are caught in stillwaters

lakes and ponds. Eels are even found in lakes with no inlet or outlet streams, so they must be able to travel overland although very few people have ever witnessed this. When they reach maturity the spawning urge overcomes them and the eels make the return journey down the rivers and across the Atlantic Ocean to spawn and die. Those eels which find their way into completely land-locked lakes sometimes find it difficult to migrate back to the sea and it is these waters where the largest eels are likely to be caught.

The average size of eel caught by anglers is about one pound (0·45 kg) but eels can grow much bigger than this. The largest eel caught by an angler in Britain weighed just over 11 lb (4·95 kg) but even larger eels have been lifted from the river bed in dredger buckets.

Baits and tackle for catching eels

Eels are extemely powerful fish and strong tackle is needed to land the larger specimens. They cannot be tired out by 'playing the fish' as can other species and they have to be 'pumped' unceremoniously toward the bank. To 'pump' a fish you lower the tip of the rod towards the water and then, without reeling in, pull back on the rod handle to raise the tip of the rod again. You reel in the line

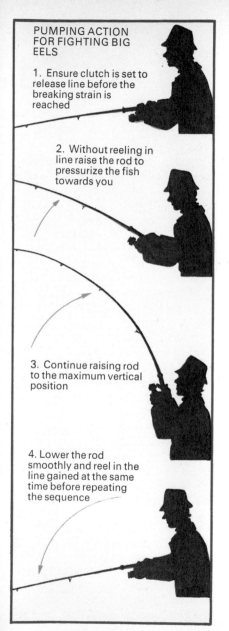

PUMPING ACTION FOR FIGHTING BIG EELS

1. Ensure clutch is set to release line before the breaking strain is reached

2. Without reeling in line raise the rod to pressurize the fish towards you

3. Continue raising rod to the maximum vertical position

4. Lower the rod smoothly and reel in the line gained at the same time before repeating the sequence

you have gained from the fish as you again lower the rod tip to repeat the 'pumping' process. Every effort should be made to keep a hooked eel coming towards you, Given half a chance the eel will wrap its body around an underwater obstruction and then you will never move it. Eels are not tackle shy and you will catch them by using very strong and even crude tackle. Some eels will actually make strong runs when hooked, but the usual tactic the eel adopts is to

An angler prepares to net a big eel. A small eel would slip through the mesh of this net

Using artery forceps to unhook an eel without removing it from the water

back away, shaking its head from side to side. This causes the line to unmistakably zig-zag.

Baits for eels are best presented on leger tackle. Most baits will catch eels, but by far the best are lobworms or small dead fish. Eels are most active during the warmer months of the year. They feed best at night or when the river is coloured after heavy rain. Eels are very adept at swallowing your bait before actually registering a bite on your tackle. It is not unusual, even when using two large lobworms as bait, to strike at the first signs of a bite, only to find when you land the eel that it has swallowed your hook right down.

When you fish for eels you get two fights, one in the water and one on the bank. Unless you want to eat your eel or to photograph it then the best idea is to reel it into the bank and then release it without touching it. If the hook is showing in the eel's mouth, hold the line tight and reach down with a pair of artery forceps and simply shake the hook loose, but if the eel has swallowed the hook cut the line as close to the eel's mouth as possible. Avoid handling the eel since you are certain to have it wrap round your arm and cover your clothes in thick slime. Don't kill an eel just for the sake of it, or because you don't like the look of them. Some anglers dislike eels but they are fun to catch and can provide the beginner with his first big fish when he is not yet skilful enough to catch other species.

Grayling

The grayling is a member of the salmon family but because it spawns at the same time of year as coarse fish it is usually regarded as such. Grayling cannot tolerate pollution and because of this their distribution is restricted to clean, fast-flowing rivers. In rivers where they exist, grayling are generally found in great numbers. In some rivers which are managed as trout waters, grayling are regarded as a pest and removed by their thousands. The extent to which grayling eat trout fry or actually compete with trout for food is very arguable, especially since most trout rivers are now artifically stocked with mature trout.

The grayling is a handsome fish with a vividly marked, sail-like dorsal fin. The eyes of the grayling are pear shaped and large. Although not long-lived, grayling grow very quickly during their first few years and can reach a length of 11 inches (27·9 cm) in 2 years. The mouth of

A brace of big grayling. Note the sail-like dorsal fin

The sail-like dorsal fin of a grayling. A cock grayling has a larger fin than a hen fish

the grayling is underneath a pointed snout and rather suggests that it is adapted to feeding on the river bed. This is somewhat misleading because grayling do rise readily to take flies from the surface of the river. Grayling spawn in early spring and the eggs are large and sticky so that they lodge in the gravel on the river bed.

Locating grayling

During the summer, when the water is warm and rivers are frequently very low, the grayling venture into the very fast shallow water where there is the most oxygen. In autumn grayling come into peak condition and can provide the trout fly angler with excellent sport after the trout season has closed. Grayling are basically a shoal fish although the individual fish which form the shoal may not be grouped closely together.

When you locate one grayling, the chances are that plenty more will be nearby.

Baits and tackle for catching grayling

One of the most enjoyable methods of catching grayling is with light, dry fly-fishing tackle. When fishing in clear rivers it is often possible to watch a grayling rise up from the river bed to take your fly. Grayling are seldom choosy about the pattern of fly you use providing it is presented correctly. If the fish are rising to a big hatch of natural fly then it is wise to use an imitation which closely resembles the natural insect. Many fancy patterns of fly are successful for catching grayling. Some of the better varieties are Green Insect, Sturdy's Fancy and White Witch. These flies are all made from similar materials. Any fly

THREE FANCY GRAYLING FLIES

Sturdy's
Fancy

Green
Insect

White
Witch

which has a white or pale hackle combined with a peacock herl body will catch grayling.

When grayling rise up to intercept surface flies they do so very differently from trout. Because the grayling's mouth is underslung it has to be in a vertical position to grab the fly. As it takes the fly, the grayling rolls forward and dives back down towards the river bed. In fast water this happens very quickly indeed but in slow glides the grayling will rise up through the water more leisurely. Grayling will also readily accept a wet fly. In colder weather when the grayling are lying in the deeper

Grayling rise from near the river bed to intercept a surface fly before turning down to their original position

Current

glides, a leaded fly will get the line down to where the fish are feeding. Leaded shrimps and nymphs are very effective.

Grayling feed right through the winter, even in the coldest weather. At this time of year fly-fishing is not very effective and the fish are best sought using float tackle. Although they are not very large fish, grayling are strong fighters especially in a fast current where they use their large dorsal fin to great advantage. When fishing close to the bank in deeper glides, a stick float trotted down using 2 to 3 lb (0·9 to 1·35 kg) breaking strain line is ideal. Begin by fishing close to the bottom and control the float so that it travels down the swim slightly slower than the current. Look for places where the faster currents run alongside pools of slower water. The grayling frequently take up position right alongside the fast water. During the autumn, grayling will be found in the shallow rippled water. The traditional bob floats advocated for catching grayling in this type of water are not very efficient. Small carrot floats have the buoyancy of a bob float but are more streamlined and offer less resistance to the current. These floats will allow you to fish in very shallow water. Let the float travel down at the speed of the current. When a grayling takes the bait the current will force your float under.

In really cold conditions worms are more attractive than maggots or redworms since they retain their wriggle. Maggots stiffen and elongate in cold water and lose their effectiveness. A good grayling hooked in a fast current fights very strongly. The fight of a grayling is

A typical northern grayling river with fast shallows and deeper glides

An angler prepares to land a big
grayling hooked on a dry fly at the head
of the pool

Gently held upside down, grayling
usually remain still long enough to be
unhooked

similar to that of an eel. The fish
lunges and twists in the strong
current. The side of a grayling's
mouth is a very thin membrane, and
fish hooked in this spot will frequently shed the hook. Unhooking
grayling is not always easy because
the fish twist and squirm so much
when you get hold of them. The best
way to hold a grayling is to grasp it
around the middle and hold it upside
down. Held like this they usually
remain still long enough to enable
you to remove the hook. In really
cold weather, grayling will still feed
but are less likely to be in the really
fast water. Laying on with float
tackle in pools at the side of the main
flow will produce fish.

Gudgeon, bleak & pope

A cloud of fine groundbait will attract hordes of gudgeon into the area you are fishing

There are a number of species which inhabit rivers and lakes which are not really large enough to offer good sport but are usually very numerous and easy to catch. The experienced angler normally tries to avoid catching them but such fish give the young angler the encouragement he needs to develop into a better angler. Most of these small fish are excellent bait fishes for large predatory fish such as pike, zander and chub.

Gudgeon

The gudgeon is often the first fish a young angler catches. They seldom grow larger than 4 oz (113·4 g) but for their size they can be enjoyable to catch. Gudgeon are shoal fish and can be caught in large numbers. A gudgeon is similar in appearance to small barbel, but has only 2 barbules instead of 4, with much larger scales than those of a small barbel.

Gudgeon are bottom feeders and thrive where the river bed is gravelly, and can also be found in lakes and gravel pits where they have been introduced.

Maggots or small worms fished on very fine float tackle is the best way to catch gudgeon. Maggots are the most convenient bait and you can often catch a number of gudgeon on the same maggot without having to rebait every cast. The bait must be on the bottom, so if you are trotting a float through a swim, adjust your tackle so you are fishing well over depth. A few handfuls of fine cloud groundbait thrown in will soon have gudgeon swarming into the area.

It takes an awful lot of gudgeon to win a fishing match so speed is essential to catch as many as this

Bleak

These little silvery fish are often referred to as willow blades. Bleak are surface feeders with a protruding lower lip. Throw in a few loose maggots and set your float tackle to fish no more than 18 in (45·7 cm) deep. Tackle should be very fine with a single maggot for hookbait. Bites from bleak can be very fast, but don't be tempted to strike hard. Should you strike hard and miss the fish, the tackle will fly out of the water, and when fishing so shallow, the hook is likely to tangle round the float. Bleak seldom weigh much more than 4 oz (113·4 g).

Pope or ruffe

More commonly known as the tommy ruffe, this little fish can be a real pest on some rivers. Unlike most small fish it has a very large mouth and is quite capable of taking a lobworm intended for larger fish. The tommy ruffe is a bottom feeder and looks rather like a miniature perch without the stripes. Ruffe can be caught very easily using worms or maggots on float and leger tackle. The ruffe has the annoying habit of clamping its mouth tightly shut and extending its gill flaps when lifted out of the water. To remove the hook, gently press the gill covers flat and it will obligingly open its mouth. Like the gudgeon and bleak, the ruffe rarely grow to a weight of more than 4 oz (113·4 g).

Above: Ruffe will often clamp their mouths shut around the hook and puff their spiky gills out

Below: To remove the hook gently close the gill covers and the ruffe will open its mouth

Perch

Perch were once the species of fish most familiar to Britain's young anglers. Disease wiped out perch in some waters and in many others they have been very slow to regain their former numbers. The slow recovery from disease is surprising because perch are extremely prolific breeders. Like the roach, perch will tolerate and adapt to all kinds of environment from ponds to fast flowing rivers.

The perch is a distinctive fish with black bands along its green flanks. The dorsal fin is large with sharp spikes on the top. The edges of the gill covers are also pointed and can stick in your hand if you handle them carelessly. When you handle a perch, gently stroke the dorsal fin down flat and keep the edge of your hand away from the pointed gill cover. Small perch feed on insect larvae and crustaceans but when they reach a certain size they become very predatory. Small to medium sized perch are shoal fish, but the very large ones lead a solitary existence.

In small ponds and lakes with a poor food supply perch may be present in large numbers but seldom grow very large. The point at which the size of the perch in the population becomes limited depends a great deal on the richness of the water. In acid waters perch seldom grow larger than 4 oz (113·4 g), but in a richer environment the fish may not become stunted until they reach a size of 12 oz (339 g). A 12 oz perch is

The spiky dorsal fin of a perch

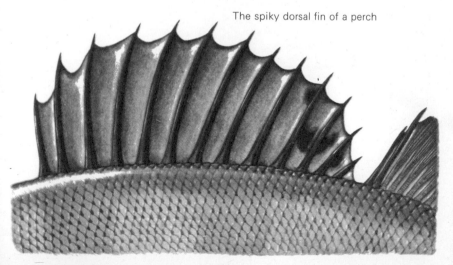

not very large but at least it is large enough to offer good sport when hooked. In waters like this there is always the outside chance that a few perch may have outgrown the rest and reached specimen size. I have known several waters where the average size of the perch has only been 12 oz but it has suddenly produced a magnificent fish of 3 lb (1·35 kg). The poor waters where perch seldom grow larger than 4 oz (113·4 g) are very unlikely to produce any bigger fish. Small perch are easy to catch and are splendid for building up the confidence of the young angler. Perch seem to be almost oblivious to clumsy casting or

Small perch are easy to catch but larger ones such as these fine fish are more difficult

the bad presentation of tackle.

Perch spawn in early spring and the eggs are laid amongst reed stems or the feathery roots of bankside trees which grow into the water. Perch eggs are laid in long, thread-like ribbons which are woven in and out of the reed stems. In appearance they are not unlike the ribbons of toad spawn.

Locating perch

Perch like lots of cover and will congregate near weeds or water lily beds. Therefore, in rivers, fish near weedbeds or beds of bulrushes. Failing this try the lengths of river which are heavily overgrown with willow bushes or where trees have fallen in and been washed up against the banking. During the summer, masses of tiny fry will congregate around these and perch will not be far away. Gaps in thick weedbeds are good spots to locate shoal perch.

Baits and tackle for catching perch

On hot, sunny days you can often get the perch feeding madly by baiting up a gap in the weeds with maggots. Begin by feeding a few loose maggots into the gaps in the weed. If the water is clear and you are using Polaroid sunglasses you may even see the perch leave the weedbed and begin intercepting the slowly sinking maggots. Use a 12 foot (3.64 metre) float rod with a small quill float attached

Perch can be found close to the bank especially if there are plenty of rushes and weed

to the line by float rubbers at the top and the bottom. Lightly shot the float with most of the weight immediately below the float. Throw in a few loose maggots followed by your float tackle. The perch will swarm through the gaps intercepting the falling maggots, including those on your hook. These tactics work equally well when fishing at close range in both rivers and lakes. In rivers, laying on over depth next to near-bank weed-beds works well in late summer and autumn. Worms are also an excellent perch bait, especially a large, lively lobworm. Large perch will often lurk amongst bulrush beds, and a lob-worm trotted down with the current next to these will tempt the perch out into the open to grab the worm.

Legering will catch perch and is often the only way of presenting a bait next to submerged tree trunks or alongside banking reinforcement stakes. When legering with a big bait, such as a lobworm or a dead fish, always allow the perch to run with the bait a little way before striking. In a sluggish river, mount the rod on 2 rod rests raised well above the ground. Mould a dough bobbin on to the line between the first 2 rod rings and pull this down to the ground. When the dough bobbin begins to move up towards the rod, lift the rod from the rest and move it forward slightly. This will allow the fish to run further before the dough bobbin wedges in the rod ring and the fish feels any resistance. As the line tightens, strike firmly and smoothly. In fast flowing water the best method for detecting bites is touch legering. As you feel the draw on the line when a perch picks up your bait, move the rod forward so that the fish can take line before you strike. When legering small, dead fish baits hold the rod, and if no bites are forthcoming reel in a couple of turns. The sudden movement sometimes induces a perch to grab the bait. Most small fish will attract perch. Minnows are easy to obtain but are unlikely to catch bigger perch than when lobworms are used. Small roach and gudgeon make better perch baits. When using fish baits don't use a wire trace or treble hooks. Large perch are sure to

A liphooked minnow will catch plenty of perch

reject a bait presented in this way.

Spinning is an active way of catching perch, and by using spinning tackle you can search a lot of water. Perch will take many kinds of spinner, such as a mepps or Devon minnow. Don't be in a rush to lift the spinner from the water as perch will frequently follow it right to the bank and grab hold at the last possible moment.

In winter perch will move into the deeper water. In rivers perch may be found congregated in large shoals away from the full force of the current. Big perch are impressive fish and are strong fighters. Even perch of around half a pound (0·22 kg) put up a tremendous fight for their size. For some reason perch have never captured the imagination of anglers in the way that roach have. Perch are every bit as colourful as roach and certainly fight a lot harder when hooked.

Pike

Pike have long been the subject of folklore and myths, and are subject to more misconceptions than any other species. The stories told about pike which slaughter ducks or that attack dogs and bathers are endless. Most of these tales are simply superstitious nonsense. I well remember netting a lake which the locals claimed was full of monster pike that supposedly attacked flocks of Canada geese on the water. The final score after netting the whole lake 3 times was 17 pike, the largest of which weighed only 3 lb (1·35 kg).

A large predatory fish, the pike feeds by charging into a shoal of fish, then seizing the one that is slowest in dashing out of its way. The large flattened mouth and sharp teeth of the pike are perfect for seizing hold of smaller fish. The pike is beautifully streamlined, with a large tail and the dorsal fin placed far back along its body. Pike have a tremendous burst of speed from being stationary, but seldom chase their prey over long distances. The teeth of a pike are hinged to fold back towards its throat, so it is a one-way journey for any fish seized by a pike. Pike usually grab their prey across the middle and turn them to swallow them head first.

As soon as the head of the fish enters the pike's throat, very strong digestive juices begin to work. When pike tackle large prey, the head of the victim will be partly digested whilst the tail will still be dangling from the corner of the pike's mouth. Pike will drag down and eat small ducklings paddling across the surface of the water, but it is not a regular occurrence. I have done a lot of pike

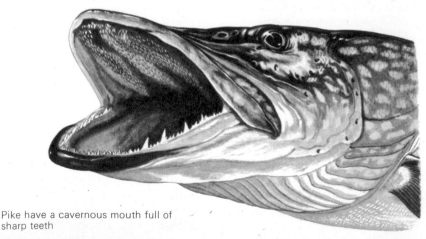

Pike have a cavernous mouth full of sharp teeth

Pike will lie amongst cover and charge into a shoal of roach which ventures close

fishing and never once seen this happen. It has been said that pike will not attack tench but this is not true either. The eyes on a pike are positioned near the top of its head so it can observe the water above more easily than the water below. Being bottom feeders, tench are probably not so easily noticed by pike as are midwater feeders.

The distribution of pike is widespread both in Britain and Europe. Often pike are the only species of coarse fish to inhabit fast-flowing, cold, game rivers. Where the pike's prey is limited to salmon and trout the predators can grow very large. In suitable waters pike can grow to a weight of 50 lb (22·5 kg). The average size of pike is well below this

weight and in many waters a pike weighing more than 15 lb (6·75 kg) is a splendid fish. Pike spawn very early in the year, well before most other species of coarse fish. By the time the fry of the other species have hatched and are shoaled in vast numbers, the tiny pike will have grown large enough to feed on them. Pike are solitary fishes and are widely distributed in river and lake systems, but concentrations of them will occur in favoured areas. It is no coincidence that where large numbers of pike are to be found, there are vast numbers of other species on which the pike feed.

(*Inset*) A roach mounted on standard snap tackle for pike fishing

Baits and tackle for catching pike

Anglers continually hooking and landing dace or roach may experience a pike grabbing hold of a hooked fish. The pike are attracted by the struggles of the hooked fish. Fish held in keepnets are a big attraction for pike. It is not at all unusual to glance down at your net to see a pike lying with its snout pressed against the mesh. Hungry pike will even grab hold of the net with their mouths and thrash about in a frantic effort to get at the occupants. Pike which are behaving like this are easy to catch. Mount a deadbait on to a wire trace and gently lower it into the general area in which you saw the pike. You should not have long to wait for the pike to appear and snap at your bait. Don't delay the strike as the fish will often turn and swallow the bait quickly. If the water is clear you may be able to watch the pike puffing its gills out as it attempts to swallow the bait.

Locating pike

Pike will frequently patrol the edges of weedbeds or the vicinity of submerged branches or debris in rivers. Occasionally pike will feed madly and locating them is no problem. A pike charging into a shoal of roach feeding near the surface will cause the small fish to scatter in panic, often jumping out of the water.

The timing of the strike depends a great deal on the size of fish you are using as bait. When using a small roach or gudgeon, strike immediately and the chances are you will hook your pike. Wait slightly longer if using a larger bait such as a small chub, although it is sometimes difficult to judge the timing correctly. There are occasions when a pike will pick up a bait and just swim around with the fish held in the front of its mouth. When pike are behaving in this manner it is often wise to use small fish baits. A pike which is not really hungry may attempt to swallow a small bait whilst only 'playing' with a larger one. When a pike has taken your bait, take up all the slack line before striking to drive the hooks home. Strike smoothly but firmly.

Striking into a pike is one of the most exciting moments in angling because you are never sure whether it will be a 2 lb (0·9 kg) fish or a 20 lb (9 kg) fish.

Use a large landing net for pike and not a gaff. Gaffs are poles ending in large hooks which can damage a fish unnecessarily. Wait until the pike is fully played out before drawing it over the waiting net. When using two treble hooks on snap tackle, try and see on which of them the fish is hooked. If the top one is loose and dangling from the pike's mouth be very careful that it doesn't tangle in the mesh of the landing net before the pike is in it. Don't be tempted to lift a small pike out of the water by grasping it across the back of its head when landing a

A hooked pike is drawn over the net

The fish makes a final attempt to escape

Above: Four young anglers display the results after fishing with experienced pike anglers

Below: A gag keeps the pike's jaws apart for unhooking. To prevent damage the prongs of the gag are padded

fish from a boat. The pike is liable to begin shaking its head and a loose treble hook may become impaled in your hand. Do not be worried about the task of unhooking a pike. Wrap the fish in a wet cloth, leaving the head clear, and lay it on the ground. Kneel *astride* the fish – not on it – so that its body is supported against your legs. This way the fish is unable to bounce about. Insert a gag into the pike's mouth to hold it open and gently remove the hooks with a pair of long nosed artery forceps. Providing you do not put your hands into the pike's mouth you will not be bitten.

Pike are edible, but they are something of an acquired taste. Unless you want to take the fish for eating, return it quickly to the water. Large pike are useless for eating and these should be returned alive.

Roach

The roach has a widespread distribution and there are very few types of water where roach will not thrive. Roach are so adaptable that they are equally at home in a small farm pond or a fast-flowing chalk stream. There can be no other species of fish which is so adaptable to different habitats. The roach is one of the most popular fish with anglers, and part of its popularity must stem from the fact that very few waters are without roach. The roach is not a big fish and most anglers are pleased at catching one weighing a pound (0·45 kg). The largest record roach in Britain weighed 4 lb 1 oz (1·8 kg) but this fish was full of spawn. Very few roach over 3 lb (1.35 kg) are recorded each year and the lifetime's ambition of most anglers is a 2 lb (0·9 kg) fish.

The beginner may confuse roach and rudd, and to complicate matters these species interbreed readily in waters containing them both. The rudd is a much deeper-bodied fish, having more vivid colouration than the roach. The two most reliable differences are that the dorsal fin of the rudd is set further along the back than that of the roach, and also the lower lip of the rudd projects strongly, indicating a surface feeding fish. The dorsal fin on the roach begins just behind the front of the pelvic fin. The position of the dorsal fin on a rudd is much further back relative to the pelvic fin. Roach will

COMPARISON BETWEEN ROACH AND RUDD

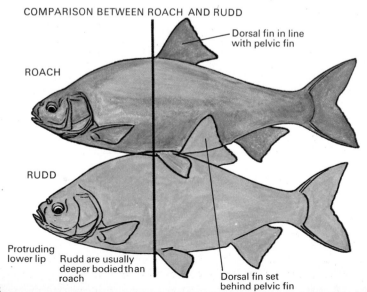

Dorsal fin in line with pelvic fin

ROACH

RUDD

Protruding lower lip

Rudd are usually deeper bodied than roach

Dorsal fin set behind pelvic fin

Roach like these two superb fish are popular with Britain's anglers

also interbreed with bream in some waters but these are much easier to distinguish than roach/rudd hybrids. The roach/bream hybrids are much deeper fish than a true roach and the anal fin is very much longer than that of a true roach.

Roach will feed freely throughout the year and can be caught in the severest of winter weather. Early summer roach are often in poor condition after spawning. The male fish feel rough to touch and are covered in tiny spawning tubercles. Roach are shoal fish and small roach will move about in really vast shoals. As the fish grow larger, the size of these shoals diminishes as predators such as pike and eels take their toll.

Locating roach

During the summer months river roach are likely to be found in the faster, well oxygenated water. Weir pools and gravelly shallows are likely holding areas. In lakes, roach will move into the shallows where there is most weed. Roach will feed at any depth, and in water with abundant fly life they will feed on surface flies that are hatching. I have seen roach taking mayflies as eagerly as any trout.

The amount of light plays a very important part in the feeding behaviour of roach, especially the larger fish. On bright sunny days it is noticeable that the larger roach begin feeding in the evening when

The well oxygenated water of a weirpool attracts shoals of roach during the summer

the light starts to fail. Even on cloudy days the roach will become more active towards late afternoon when the light is 'softer'. Small roach can be caught at almost any time of day, as can the small fish of most species. The clarity of the water affects the amount of light penetrating through the water and this should also be taken into account. Some lakes are stream fed and in times of heavy rain the stream will wash suspended silt into the lake, causing the water to become coloured. This will reduce the visibility in the water and will often encourage the roach to feed madly even on very bright days. The most difficult of all waters in which to catch good roach consistently are those gravel pits which are heavily weeded and remain clear. Late evenings are easily the most productive times on these waters. It is often worth staying at the waterside for a couple of hours after dark. On rivers, the roach still feed best in poor light, so again evening is often the most productive time. On some of the larger rivers the wash from boats discolours the water, encouraging roach to feed when the boating activity has subsided. In winter, roach are much more likely to be found in the deeper parts of rivers and still waters.

Baits and tackle for catching roach

To enjoy the most sport from roach the tackle should be fine and deli-
cate. For float fishing, use a 12 foot (3·64 metre) rod and a fixed-spool reel loaded with a 2 lb (0·9 kg) breaking strain line. When legering increase the reel line to 3 lb (1·35 kg) breaking strain. When lake fishing at reasonably close range use a slim line antenna float or a bodied waggler. Place the bulk of the shot under the float so that the bait will fall slowly through the water. This will sometimes catch fish 'on the drop' but, if no bites occur as the bait is sinking, will present a bait on the lake bed.

Maggots and casters on a size 16 or 18 hook will catch lots of roach but are not the ideal bait for attracting the larger fish. A single grain of sweetcorn is a good roach bait, and using these you are unlikely to be pestered by the small roach. Bread used as flake or paste is also an excellent roach bait. The only problem when using bread flake in a flowing river is that when you retrieve the tackle after trotting the swim the flake is liable to fall off the hook. This means you are constantly rebaiting, but bread is such a good roach bait that it is worth the effort. During the summer months, seed baits are deadly for roach. When using tares, feed the swim very sparingly with grains of hemp. Seed baits are all very filling so don't overfeed or the fish will stop biting. On many waters small knobs of cheese moulded round a size 12 hook are an excellent roach bait.

Big roach are less inclined to chase a bait than are the smaller fish so you

These roach show signs of keepnet damage – split fins, red bellies and missing scales

need to present a static bait to catch these. In a lake use an antenna float but present a larger bait so that it is resting on the lake bed. For long range lake fishing, leger a larger bait and detect bites by using a swing tip. In a river, legering will usually catch the larger roach. During the winter months, laying on with float tackle next to the near bank is also a productive method. Small roach may be quick biting, but the larger fish will normally give slow deliberate bites when you are presenting them with a fair sized offering. A number of the really large roach which have been caught have fallen to king-sized baits intended for larger species. The record roach fell to a lobworm intended to catch tench.

Roach are very easily damaged by keepnets. If large numbers of roach are crammed together in too small a net, their bellies rub on the mesh and become red and sore. The scales are easily dislodged and their fins will tear and split. Use a large knotless keepnet and at the end of the day release the fish by lowering the mouth of the net and letting the fish swim out.

Roach should be released by lowering the mouth of the net into the water and allowing the fish to swim out

Rudd

The rudd is more of a stillwater fish than the roach, and is not frequently found in flowing rivers. The exception to this is in Ireland where rudd are sometimes found in rivers with a strong current. If anything, the rudd is a more handsome fish than the roach. The protruding lower lip of the rudd enables it to feed easily on the surface.

Locating rudd

When they are feeding on the surface during warm weather, locating rudd is easy. The surface will become a mass of ripples as the fish feed on hatching insects. Larger rudd will roll noisily on the surface, frequently giving a glimpse of their golden flanks. If there is no obvious sign of surface activity throw a few pieces of bread crust on to the lake surface and let the wind carry these out. As soon as rudd encounter the bread they will begin tearing it to pieces, giving away their location. In vast gravel pits the rudd are just as likely to be far out in open water as they are to be next to reed beds and long casting is often necessary to reach the shoal.

Baits and tackle for catching rudd

Tackle employed for catching rudd should be similar to that used for roach. For casting long distances to

The protruding lower lip of the rudd

catch surface-feeding rudd use a heavy bodied waggler float and place all the shot next to the float. The tackle will be heavy enough to cast far out into the lake yet the waggler float is sensitive enough to register the bites. By placing all the shot immediately below the float the bait is allowed to sink slowly through the shoal of feeding fish. Fish taking the bait as it is sinking will either cause the float to rise quickly from the surface, or tow it along the surface. When you strike, move the rod right back over your shoulder to ensure you drive the hook home. A long, sweeping strike is essential to take up the slack line when fishing at long range, and also to compensate for any stretch in the nylon.

Rudd are prolific breeders and, where they exist, can be caught in large numbers

Maggots and casters will catch plenty of rudd. Bread is a good bait but where hordes of little rudd are present, flake will be whittled away very quickly. Catching big rudd and avoiding the small fish is a very difficult problem. Sometimes the shoal will form with the small rudd just below the surface whilst the larger fish lurk deeper down. To get a bait down to the larger fish, place the bulk of the shot far enough below your float to drag the bait quickly through the hordes of tiddler rudd. Catching large rudd is usually a problem of location because on many waters rudd are so prolific that they become stunted. The best places for big rudd are gravel pits, large lakes and slow moving fenland rivers.

In winter the rudd will feed on the bottom and can be caught using roach tactics. Rudd will still readily move up through the water to intercept the loose feed and groundbait as it slowly sinks. If this happens, shot the float so that you are fishing on the drop (see page 52) and strike at any unusual movement of the float.

Tench

Female. Fins smaller and daintier

Male. Pelvic fins large and spoonlike

Although a few tench are found in flowing rivers, they are basically a fish of lakes and ponds. The tench is a beautiful olive-green fish with large powerful fins and tiny red eyes. Tench are a summer fish although a few are caught each winter. Tench are the one species where it is easy to distinguish between the males and females. The male tench have very large, spoon-like pelvic fins. The muscles around the base of these fins are also large, giving the fish a very lumpy appearance.

Tench can be found in huge shoals and some very big catches can be taken. In a number of small weedy lakes, tench fishing can be very easy. The tench in this type of water are unlikely to grow very large but when you consider that small tench weigh between one and two pounds (0·45 to 0·9 kg) some hectic sport can be enjoyed. In larger lakes and gravel pits, tench may not be so prolific but

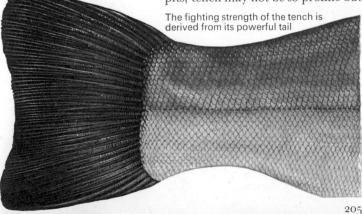

The fighting strength of the tench is derived from its powerful tail

they grow to a good size. The record tench from a British water stands at 10 lb 1 oz (4·6 kg) but larger fish have been caught suffering from dropsy (a disease where the fluids accumulate in body tissues). Tench are prone to this disease and become very bloated, resembling a football with fins.

Tench are very powerful fighters and are one of the most popular species with anglers during the summer months. They require very high water temperatures to spawn successfully and in many lakes do not spawn until July or even early August. In high altitude lakes the tench may not spawn every year if the summer is a cool one. One of the peculiarities of tench is that very small specimens are rarely caught. This is probably because the tiny tench live amongst the thick weed beds. It is certainly unusual on most waters to catch a tench weighing less than one pound (0·45 kg). June is definitely the best month for tench fishing since they have seldom spawned by early June and the fish are fat and healthy. This

Tench feeding on a silty lake bed stir up the bottom and release bubbles

is the time of year when some really exceptional tench are caught. When tench begin spawning the fish do not feed, but as soon as spawning is completed the fish are likely to go on a feeding spree.

Locating tench

Locating feeding tench in a small lake or pond is not very difficult especially if the water is fairly shallow. Large numbers of tench feeding on the bottom discolour the water. Tench grubbing around on a silted bottom create masses of tiny bubbles which rise to the surface in clusters. Pre-baiting with lots of groundbait will attract tench into a swim. Concentrate the groundbait, rather than spreading it around. If weed-beds are nearby, lay trails of ground-bait from the weedbeds to the main area. Tench are often associated with a thick, muddy bottom but in reality they prefer a fine gravel or silt. The most favoured conditions of all for tench is a gravel bed covered with a layer of soft silt.

Baits and tackle for catching tench

When you discover a lake bed of this nature, put all your groundbait in before you tackle up. Mix dry bread-crumb into balls by soaking in water, and liberally fill these balls of ground-bait with maggots by moulding the ball into a cup shape to enclose them. Throw the balls of groundbait into the area you intend to fish. The groundbait will break up and cover the bottom but the maggots will quickly burrow into the layer of silt. The maggots are unable to burrow very deep because of the hard gravel below the layer of silt. Tench attrac-ted to the area by the groundbait soon gobble this up but whilst doing so waft some of the maggots out of the silt with the movement of their fins. Once they have discovered lots of maggots in the silt the tench will spend a long time digging for them. I have had tench feeding continuously for 12 hours after pre-baiting in this manner. Early season tench are not usually selective over bait but mag-gots, lobworms, breadflake and sweetcorn are probably the best baits. If small fish or other species are present it is advisable to avoid maggots. Should a large shoal of tench move into your swim, however, the small fish will most likely move out so you can safely use maggots.

In early summer, tench will feed in very shallow water but as the months pass they will gradually move into the deeper areas. Tench will feed at all hours of the day but there is no doubt that early mornings are the best. Much depends on the weather. In heatwave conditions the feeding activity may only last a few hours, but on overcast days the fish may well feed throughout the day. When tench are feeding over a small area which you have laced with maggots, do not expect runaway bites. The tench do not have to move to find more food so your tackle has to be finely adjusted. Wherever possible use an antenna float and set the tackle so that the bait is just touching the bottom of the lake. If the float then lifts slightly or dips under, strike immediately. In the past, a great deal has been written about tench playing with the bait before actually taking it. If you wait for the float to sail away, you will either deeply hook the fish or it will have swallowed your bait and bitten through the line with its pharangeal (throat) teeth. If you are legering at long range and experience these twitches on your dough bobbin or swing tip, strike at any movement.

When you fish for tench take a dry cloth with you to wipe your hands because tench are covered with a thick layer of slime. Don't use the cloth to handle the tench because this slime protects the fish and should not be removed. Always handle fish with wet hands. This will help to prevent your hands becoming covered with slime. You will also find that, when you have landed a tench, small globules of slime will have stuck to your line near the hook. Remove all these before you rebait.

The tackle you use for tench depends on the type of water you are fishing. For float fishing in small lakes and close range fishing in gravel pits a 12 foot (3.65m) float rod is ideal. Use a line of 4lb (1.8kg) breaking strain as this will deal with most tench in open water. When legering at long range, or if the water you are fishing is full of

Early morning on the first day of the season and a good tench is played towards the net
Right: A good tench catch with one solitary roach

water lilies and weed, use a carp rod and 6 lb (2·7 kg) breaking strain line.

Sport with tench usually ends with the first hard frosts in late October or early November.

Trout

There are two common trout species, the brown trout and the rainbow trout. The brown trout is native to Britain and Europe whilst the rainbow trout was introduced from America towards the end of the nineteenth century. Rainbow trout do not breed naturally in British rivers and lakes so stocks rely almost entirely on hatchery reared fish. Rainbow trout can grow very large and fish weighing more than 30 lb (13·5 kg) have been reared in fish farms. Producing fish of this size is expensive so most trout fisheries stock their rivers with rainbow trout weighing between 1 and 2 lb (0·45 to 0·90 kg). The name rainbow implies a highly colourful fish, but in fact rainbow trout are often less colourful than the brown trout. When in peak condition the rainbow trout is not very colourful at all, having a distinct silvery appearance. It is when approaching spawning condition that the rainbow trout takes on the

This young angler has every right to look pleased as he holds a sizeable brown trout

colours which gave it its name. The male fish especially become very dark, almost black, with a vivid red or pink band running along the length of the body. The spots or speckles on the rainbow trout are small and spread along the body to cover the fins and tail.

The colouration of the brown trout can vary tremendously even on those fish caught from the same stretch of river. Some brown trout are covered in speckles whilst others have only a few large spots around the gill covers and along the back. The spots on the brown trout are larger than those on the rainbow and have a white or pale halo surrounding them. Very few, if any, spots are found on the tail of a brown trout. Brown trout which have lived in a river for a long time often have a yellow or gold tint to their flanks and belly. The spots on the rainbow trout can be black or red.

Trout are not a shoal fish although groups of rainbow trout may often be located feeding together in a reservoir. In a river, trout require cool, well-oxygenated water and are usually found only in the middle and upper reaches. Brown trout spawn at a different time of year to coarse fish. The eggs are laid amongst the gravel between November and January and may take up to 12 weeks to hatch. The female trout will make a hollow in the fine gravel by wafting her tail. This hollow is known as a redd, and the eggs are laid in this, and then covered over with fine gravel. Brown trout do not normally grow as large as rainbow trout but, in some very large rich lakes, specimens can reach a weight of 20 lb (9 kg). In fast-flowing spate rivers a brown trout of 2 lb (0·9 kg) is a good fish and the average size is likely to be only 12 oz (340 g). Although brown trout will breed freely in a river, angling pressure is usually so high that the stocks have to be maintained by introducing fish reared in hatcheries. Trout will feed on almost anything from surface flies to small fish. They are greedy fish and at times very easy to catch. This is why most trout fishing is restricted to fly only and a limit placed on the number of fish you can take home. Without these restrictions most waters would soon have their trout population removed by anglers.

Locating trout

In a river, trout will usually be found in the faster water or in the shallow tail of a pool. When there is a big hatch of fly, the trout will position themselves just below the surface, rising to suck in the flies as they float past. Trout do not like high water temperatures and in the summer months will often feed best towards the evening. During the summer the shallows will be full of tiny coarse fish fry and minnows. Trout will venture into very shallow water to chase these tiny fish often creating a big bow wave on the surface as they charge about. Wading in a river is often

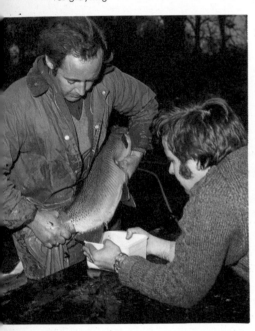

Below: Workers at the trout hatchery strip ripe eggs from a large hen rainbow trout
Below right: The upper reaches of a rocky trout river. In the autumn, fly anglers fish for grayling

trout will come in very close to the bank. When you are fishing from a boat on a reservoir, seek out the wind lanes. Wind blowing across the sur-

necessary to enable you to present a fly to a trout. Do not wade along the river unless you must. Clumsy wading frightens trout and you will scare many more fish than you catch.

In a large, featureless reservoir locating trout can sometimes be difficult. If a wind is blowing, it is best to fish into the wind, which will carry hatching insects to one side of the reservoir and the trout will congregate in this area. It is not always easy casting into the wind but you will not have to cast far, since the face of a lake does not do so evenly. Narrow channels can be seen where the effect of the wind on the surface layer is greatest. These wind lanes are the places where most of the insect life will be carried along by the surface drift, attracting trout to the area.

Baits and tackle for catching trout

On some rivers worm fishing for trout is allowed. The best type of worms are brandlings or gilt tails. To enjoy the most sport use a 12 foot (3·65 metre) float rod and 3 lb (1·35 kg) breaking strain line. In small pools, position yourself at the head of the pool and cast your float into the main flow. Allow your float tackle to be carried down at the speed of the current. Many trout rivers have a rocky bed, so set your float so that you are fishing just clear of the rocks. If the water is shallow use a carrot float but for deeper swims use a buoyant avon or balsa float. Stick floats work well in the smooth glides, but in turbulent water they are not buoyant enough and will be dragged under if you try to hold your tackle back in the current. Use a size 14 barbless hook and then you will be able to return any undersize trout without damaging them. Any trout you want to take home for eating should be killed quickly and cleanly with a blow to the back of the head. Don't put dead trout in a polythene bag and leave them on the bank because if it is sunny they will quickly 'go off' and lose their flavour. Never be tempted to kill more trout than you actually need for eating.

Zander

The zander, or pike-perch as it is often called, is a large predatory fish. The zander is a member of the same group of fish as the perch and has a similar dorsal fin formation along its back. Like the perch, zander are shoal fish and when you catch one the chances are you will catch more. Unlike the perch, zander have some very sharp teeth. In Britain, zander are only present in waters where they have been recently introduced such as the slow-flowing fenland rivers of East Anglia. The zander introduced to East Anglia grew quickly and bred successfully so that they are now firmly established in this area. The vast network of rivers and drains in this region are all connected so they have been able to spread rapidly.

Zander are unable to eat really large fish so they prey on the vast shoals of roach and bream fry. The best way of locating zander in a slow-flowing fenland river is to first locate large concentrations of fry. The shoals of zander which feed on these are unlikely to be far away.

Baits and tackle for catching zander

Whilst a few very small zander are caught on maggots and worms the best methods for catching zander are livebaiting, deadbaiting and spinning. Deadbaiting has proved to be a very effective method for catching zander but eels can be a nuisance, especially towards dusk and after dark.

The mouth of the zander is much smaller than that of a pike but it is full of sharp teeth

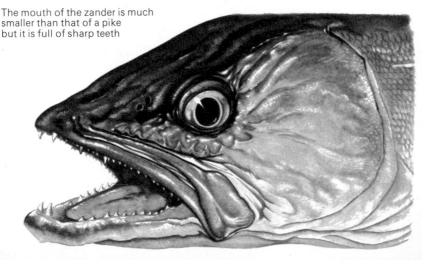

Zander are introduced predators to Britain which have colonized East Anglian rivers

Even if the eel is too small to swallow the bait it will often bite lumps out of it. Dusk is, however, one of the best times for catching zander so when deadbaiting there is very little you can do to present a deadbait which is immune from the attentions of eels. One way to get your own back is to use eels as bait for zander! A 2 inch (5 cm) chunk of eel makes a very effective zander bait.

Zander will run with a deadbait, often at great speed, before attempting to swallow it. Timing the strike is not always easy. Too soon and the fish will not be hooked, too late and the zander will have gorged the bait. Pike will often accept a bait intended

for zander which further complicates matters. The angler, giving what he imagines to be a zander plenty of time to run with the bait, sometimes ends up playing a pike which has had plenty of time to gorge the bait and is deeply hooked. Judgement of when to strike at a zander run can only be learned from experience and it is invevitable that when zander fishing a few deeply hooked pike will be caught.

Zander are good to eat and in Europe they are a popular food fish. Zander can reach a weight of over 20 lb (9 kg) but the average size is between three and five pounds (1·35 and 2·25 kg).

Useful addresses

The Salmon and Trout Association

This is the national organization for game fishermen and conservationists. The association works closely with Water Authorities for the improvement and protection of rivers especially those which contain game fish such as trout and salmon. The association has many active branches throughout the British Isles. Details of membership and subscription rates can be obtained from the Secretary, Salmon and Trout Association, Fishmongers Hall, London EC4.

The National Federation of Anglers (N.F.A.)

This organization was founded to protect, improve and promote coarse fishing in the British Isles. This body is consulted by Water Authorities and government bodies in matters affecting coarse fishing. The N.F.A. is also instrumental in organizing big fishing matches, notably the National Championships. The N.F.A. is an affiliation of angling clubs and associations so there is no individual membership. Information about the N.F.A. can be obtained from the Chief Executive, Haig House, Green Lane, Derby.

National Anglers Council (N.A.C.)

This body was formed in 1966 to promote and protect the interests of all anglers whether sea anglers, coarse fishermen or game fishermen. The N.A.C. has a free advisory service and is equipped to offer advice on most matters concerning angling. Membership is for clubs or individuals. Details of the N.A.C. can be obtained from The Secretary, National Anglers Council, 5, Cowgate, Peterborough PE1 1LR.

Water Authorities

In England a rod licence is needed wherever you fish. These are issued by the regional Water Authorities through tackle shops. Licences are only valid in the area controlled by the regional water authority. Some authorities have a minimum age under which no licence is required. This age varies from region to region and is listed with the addresses of the relevant water authorities.

Anglian Water Authority

Diploma House, Grammar School Walk, Huntingdon, Cambridgeshire PE18 6NZ. Minimum age 12. Concessionary rates age 12 to 15.

Northumbrian Water Authority

Northumbria House, Regent Centre, Gosforth, Newcastle upon Tyne NE3 3PX. Concessionary rates under 16.

North West Water Authority

New Town House, Buttermarket Street, Warrington WA1 2QG. Minimum age 14. Concessionary rates age 14 to 16.

Severn Trent Water Authority

Abelson House, 2297 Coventry Road, Sheldon, Birmingham B26

3PR. Minimum age 14.

Southern Water Authority
Guildbourne House, Chatsworth Road, Worthing, Sussex. Concessionary rates under 16.

South West Water Authority
3/5 Barnfield Road, Exeter EX1 1RE. Minimum age 10. Concessionary rates age 10 to 16.

Thames Water Authority
2nd Floor, Reading Bridge House, Reading, Berkshire RG1 8PR. Minimum age 16.

Welsh National Water Development Authority
Cambrian Way, Brecon, Powys. Concessionary rates for juveniles under 16.

Wessex Water Authority
Techno House, Redcliffe Way, Bristol BS1 6NY. Minimum age 11. Half price age 11 to 16.

Yorkshire Water Authority
West Riding House, 67 Albion Street, Leeds LS1 5AR. Minimum age 14.

Glossary

Anti-reverse lever Small lever or catch on a fixed spool reel which when engaged prevents the reel from being wound backwards.

Arlesey bomb A pear-shaped leger weight with a swivel, through which the line passes, attached at the pointed end.

Artery forceps Long nosed pincers for removing the larger size of hook from a fish's mouth.

Bobbin indicator A device for detecting bites whilst legering. The bobbin is attached to the line between the first two rod rings. When a fish bites the bobbin rises towards the rod.

Brandlings Small worms found in compost heaps. Distinguished from other worms by yellow and red bands around their bodies.

Breaking strain The manufacturers' estimate of the dry strength of the line. This will decrease when the line is wet and knotted. Also decreases with age.

Centre pin reel The original type of fishing reel consisting of a circular drum on to which the line is directly wound. A superb reel for controlled float fishing in a flowing river.

Closed-face fixed-spool reel Similar in design to a standard fixed-spool reel but the spool and winding mechanism are shrouded in a casing.

Close season Fishing for coarse fish is not allowed in England and Wales from March 15th to June 15th. (These dates may vary according to local bylaws.) The close seasons in England and Wales for the following species are: salmon, November 1st–January 31st; trout, October 1st–February 28th. All dates are inclusive.

Coarse fish The term given to species of freshwater fish not belonging to the salmon and trout family.

Cocktail bait A combination of two baits attached to the hook together. A common example is maggot and worm cocktail.

Deadbaiting Fishing for predatory fish with dead fish as bait. Mostly used for pike and eel fishing.

Disgorger An implement for gently removing the hook from a fish's mouth.

Dry fly An artificial fly fished on a greased line so that it floats on the water surface.

Dubbing needle A strong needle used in fly-tying as an aid for tying half hitch knots, separating hackles and varnishing fly heads.

Fixed-spool reel The most widely used reel in angling today. The line is picked up by a bale arm mechanism and wound on to a spool at the front of the reel.

Floatant An oil or chemical used in fly-fishing to improve the floating qualities of a fly or line.

Float fishing Method of presenting

a bait which is suspended below a float. The float acts as a very sensitive bite indicator and by altering the distance between the float and the hook, a bait can be presented at any depth.

Fly-fishing Method of fishing with an artificial fly, usually, but not always, in the pursuit of game fish such as trout and salmon.

Freelining Similar to legering but no weight is used. The hook is tied directly to the reel line and the bait is cast out and allowed to sink naturally.

Gilt tails Small stiff red worms with yellow tips to the tails.

Groundbait Used to attract fish to the area being fished and to encourage them to feed. Groundbait can be in the form of soaked breadcrumbs or samples of the hookbait.

Hackle pliers Delicate clamps for winding on feathers to form the hackles of a dry fly.

Hook length Length of nylon line on to which the hook is whipped. The hook length should be of a slightly lower breaking strain than the main reel line.

Laying on Method of presenting a stationary bait in a flowing river with float tackle. The float is adjusted so that the tackle is fishing well over depth.

Legering Method of presenting a bait on the bed of a river or lake where a lead weight is used to hold the tackle in position.

Link leger A leger weight attached to a nylon link.

Margins The edges of a river or lake.

Over depth The distance between the float and hook is greater than the depth of water.

Paternoster rig Method used to anchor the tackle in one spot as in legering but the bait is presented on a separate nylon trace above the weight.

Pinkies Maggots of the green-bottle fly.

Plug Imitation small fish used for pike, perch and zander fishing.

Pumping Method of drawing in a big fish towards the bank. The rod is raised to gain line and the line so gained is wound on to the reel as the rod is lowered.

Quiver tip Sensitive bite indicator attached to the top of the rod when legering in flowing water.

Rolling leger Spherical leger weight with a hole drilled through the centre through which the reel line is passed. Used for trundling a bait along the river bed in search of feeding fish.

Running leger Leger weight with a swivel attached. The reel line is passed through the edge of the swivel and the leger is prevented from sliding down to the hook by a split shot nipped on to the line.

Setting the drag Adjusting the clutch on a fixed-spool reel so that a fish making a sudden and powerful lunge will take line from the spool and not break the line.

Setting the float Moving the float along the line so that the distance between the float and hook is such that the bait is being presented at the required depth. The float should stand upright or 'cock' immediately after being cast if the weighting of the line and the distance between the hook and the float are correct.

Snap tackle Two treble hooks fixed to a wire trace. Used for mounting a livebait or deadbait when pike fishing.

Spigot ferrules Tapered joints for connecting rod sections.

Spinner Revolving artificial lure used for catching predatory fish.

Split shot Small spherical lead pellets for weighting the line.

Squatts Maggots of the housefly.

Stop shot Split shot nipped on to the line to fix a leger weight the required distance from the hook.

Stret pegging A similar method to laying on. The float is set to fish over depth and a large shot is placed near the hook so that it is lying on the river bed. By raising the rod the tackle can be moved slowly downstream.

Striking Raising the rod back in response to a bite to drive the hook into the fish's mouth.

Swim Term given to the area of water being fished.

Swing tip Bite indicator used when legering in still or slow flowing waters and attached to the rod end.

Swivel A device used to prevent line twisting or kinking when spinning or legering.

Tares A seed bait sometimes called pigeon peas.

Thermocline The depth in a lake at which there is a sudden temperature drop between the warm upper layer of water and the colder deeper water during the summer months.

Through action The action of a rod which bends gradually under the strain of a fish from the rod tip right through to the handle.

Tip action The action of a rod where only the top half of the rod really bends under the pull of a fish. Tip action rods are usually used in match fishing.

Touch legering Detecting bites whilst legering by holding the line between the fingers and feeling for the bites.

Trace A length of nylon or wire attached to the reel line. In pike fishing a wire trace is used with hooks whipped on to the end of it.

Trail The distance of line between a leger weight and the bait.

Trotting A form of float fishing where the float and tackle is allowed to travel down with the stream.

Wet fly An artificial fly which is fished below the water surface.

Index